TED AND ANN

The Mystery of a Missing Child and Her Neighbor Ted Bundy

REBECCA MORRIS

Excerpts of *Ted Bundy: Conversations with a Killer* by Stephen G. Michaud and Hugh Aynesworth used with permission of the authors. (Authorlink Press, 2000).
Photograph of Louise Bundy by Russ Carmack used with permission of *The News Tribune.*
Photograph of Beverly Burr by Ellen Banner used with permission of *The Seattle Times.*
Burr family photos, letters, and poems used with permission of Beverly Burr.
Holt family photos used with permission of Sandi Holt.
Cover design by Claudia Olsen and BEAUTeBOOK.
True Books logo by Mikel Northcraft.

Published by True Books
Seattle, Washington
ISBN: 978-1484925-089
Printed in the United States of America

Praise for ***Ted and Ann***

"This is the ONLY book to read to learn the full story of the disappearance of Ann Marie Burr in August 1961. Fascinating!"

—Ann Rule
New York Times Bestselling Author

"While Ted Bundy might be the greatest evil enigma ever, author Rebecca Morris strips away the layers of the greatest mystery of his life—what was his connection to the disappearance of Ann Marie Burr? This is an astonishing achievement, the missing piece that readers of crime have long sought. Bravo for Morris!"

—Gregg Olsen
New York Times Bestselling Author

"As a journalist, I covered Ted Bundy's murder trial in 1980. Thirty years later, Rebecca Morris brings to vivid life that particular trial and the whole Bundy mystique— when a young, intelligent, charming personality hid one of the vilest hearts that ever beat. This is a chapter in American criminal history that deserves Morris' confident reporting and writing."

—Neil Chethik
Author of Father Loss:
How Sons of All Ages Come to
Terms with the Deaths of Their Dads

"Few criminals have loomed as large in the national psyche as Ted Bundy, the 'Cary Grant of serial killers,' whose string of brutal murders manages to fascinate and repulse us still. Now, in a book as chilling as it is compelling and impossible to put down, journalist Rebecca Morris presents yet another possible Bundy victim—an innocent, eight-year-old girl who disappeared from her hometown of Tacoma, Washington, in 1961, and was never found. In telling the story of Ann Marie Burr, who went missing

on a steamy August day, Morris also reveals startling, never-been-told details about Bundy's childhood, including fresh information about his illegitimacy and brief abandonment by his mother. Morris' deft writing and detailed research into Bundy's actions that summer, when he was a gangly 14-year-old roaming the Burr's neighborhood on his bike, will have you reading Ted and Ann well into the night."

—Ginger Adams Otis
Investigative Journalist

TABLE OF CONTENTS

FOR

Beverly Ann Leach Burr

January 4, 1928—September 13, 2008

"Night comes and with it the fear, the listening,
the horror again and again.
Only prayer can lessen the pain as we whisper,
'Dear God be with Ann. Please help us and other parents like us to be strong.' "

Foreword

IT HAS BEEN 50 YEARS SINCE MY BROTHER AND I were startled awake by men shining flashlights on us. It was late August, 1961, a few days before the start of school, and we were sleeping in our fort in the basement one last time. The men were police, and the scene of my parents panic and hysteria that morning is still vivid and haunting.

The tragedy described in Rebecca Morris' book, *Ted and Ann*, deeply wounded and altered my life and that of my family and others close to us. As a parent, I cannot fathom having my child taken from my home in the night. The cruelest aspect of this heinous crime is that there have been no answers. Over the years there has been a somewhat regular eruption of rumors, theories, and "confessions." None led to an answer, and all kept open a wound that never healed.

My parents' imagination must have run wild with nightmarish visions of what had or was happening to their daughter, and our family struggled to hang on to normalcy. Morris has devoted years to uncovering the details of Ann's disappearance, and the possible link to a well-known psychopath, Ted Bundy. I have learned a great deal about the time period, the facts surrounding the case, and about Ted Bundy and the other suspects in my sister's disappearance from Morris' thorough research and this book.

Our parents, trying to protect us and provide a happy childhood, shielded us from much of this even through our adult lives.

Morris spent countless hours talking with my mother, who has now passed on, as has my father. In their memory, I applaud Rebecca Morris' diligent work and skill in telling our story and the story of Ted Bundy, and I hope that it leads to answers so that even now there can be some closure. My parents, Beverly and Donald Burr, showed tremendous strength and courage in carrying on after the abduction of their oldest child. They did it for their other children. They not only managed to hold our family together, but also to nurture friendships, create beauty in their gardens, travel the world, and provide compassion and support to others who were struggling.

I was robbed of my sister, my playmate, and best friend. Some may wonder what good could come from this book if it doesn't result in answers. My hope is that it shows a family can survive an unthinkable tragedy, by finding good and beauty in life, and that the good outweighs the evil.

—Julie Burr
August, 2011

Prologue

The Day Before

SUMMER ENDED SUDDENLY ON AUGUST 30, 1961. IT was the Wednesday before Labor Day weekend, and the unusually warm weather turned muggy and the sky threatened to storm. That night, rain drenched Tacoma, Washington. Not the polite, incessant drizzle that those who live in the Pacific Northwest learn to tolerate (or they leave, and many do), but a hard rain accompanied by high winds. Trees blew down, lights went out, and neighborhoods were plunged into blackness. The wind masked any sounds that might be heard inside a house.

But in the afternoon, before the rain, it was just plain hot. Beverly Burr's steam iron made the day seem even hotter as she worked out the creases in her daughter Ann's new dress. Bev usually made her children's clothes and was so thrifty that the family teased her about it. But Ann was starting third grade, so Bev had splurged and bought the maroon-plaid jumper and butterscotch-colored blouse. Five-year-old Greg had begged for a Superman cape, so she was sewing one, although she was embarrassed for him. He'd find out the hard way on the first day of kindergarten, when none of the other children wore costumes to school.

She hadn't told her husband that she had bought Ann new school clothes, and she hoped he wouldn't notice. Bev did a lot of things she didn't tell Don. At eight-and-a-half, Ann was the eldest of four children. Mother and daughter were a lot alike: smart, independent, and stubborn, with the talent and drive to achieve something creative and remarkable in their lives. Both would be robbed of that opportunity.

During the summer of 1961, Ann often wore a paper lei she had won at the state fair (or it might have been at a function at St. Patrick's, their neighborhood parish). She liked to get up early in the morning and practice the piano. Ann hated to be called Annie, so people quickly learned not to call her that. And she wasn't known as Ann Marie, which is how the missing poster sent around the world referred to her. Just Ann.

All the children in the immediate neighborhood congregated at the Burrs'. Bev, 33 years old and the mother of four children under the age of eight, didn't work. Don, who was 35, wouldn't allow it. Bev loved to have the children at her house. She scoured magazines for games they could play and wrote stories and poems for them. Life at Bev's house could be described as wholesome.

The last children to see Ann were Susie, who lived right across the alley in back of the Burr house, and Christine, who lived a few blocks away. Ann also was good friends with a couple of teenagers, Robert Bruzas and his sister Frannie, who lived two houses east. Ann and Robert had an ongoing flirtation. She called him "lover boy," and he called her "dear" and said she was "his girl." Parents didn't question until later why a 15-year-old boy would want to spend time with an eight-year-old girl.

The children had acquaintances whom Bev didn't know, children from homes not as wholesome. Bev was naïve about the extent to which all children—hers included—got around by bicycle. Sandi Holt lived a couple of miles west of the Burrs. She was three years older than Ann but knew her. Sandi spent most of her time trailing after her older brother, Doug, and his best friend, Ted Bundy. She looked on when the boys dug tunnels or pulled pranks on other kids, but kept her distance when Ted would douse an animal with gasoline and light it on fire, or when he tried to take small girls into the woods to urinate on them.

North Tacoma was a modest neighborhood, but the houses were nice. The Burrs', on North 14th Street, just off Alder between Cedar and Junett, was a brick English bungalow built in 1934. Next door was Mrs. Gustafson's orchard, a dense landscape of apple trees and thick rows of raspberry bushes; the children, who called her "Gusty," knew all the paths between them, as well as every ditch, gulch, and abandoned home in the neighborhood. At the end of Ann's street there were open ditches 30 feet deep, courtesy of a city sewer project. At the college two blocks west, seven new dorms and fraternities were under construction and cement was being poured. The college was hurrying to get as much of the project underway before students began arriving in a few days. Everywhere there were places to play, to hide, and to be a little bit scared.

Later, Bev regretted teaching her children that the world was safe. Like most Tacoma families, she didn't know that the city's police records were full of reports of (as the police called them) "sex perverts, exhibitionists, sex oddballs, psychos, crackpots, half-wits, queers, and women with lesbian tendencies."

Ann's father didn't trust some neighbors, including the woman across the street who had spent time in the insane asylum after she had given birth to a "Negro baby." Or there was the nudist who liked to sunbathe in his backyard. The neighborhood children visited him because he gave them candy. Because of the confluence of Tacoma's port, railroad, military bases, veteran's hospital, and the insane asylum, Tacoma drew an odd and transient population.

In the summer even more strangers passed through. Just before the Labor Day weekend, neighbors noticed a man in the neighborhood selling cookware, which was strange because he didn't have any pots and pans with him. The morning paper was filled with news of the Soviet Union and the United States testing nuclear weapons; one man was getting a jump on people's fears, going door-to-door selling plans for basement bomb shelters.

That week the town was laughing about a more lighthearted story in the newspaper. A Tacoma couple was getting divorced, and the event that precipitated the split made the front page of the

Tacoma News Tribune. One night at dinner the husband gave his wife an ultimatum: she had to choose between him and her seven cats, which ate at the table with them. She chose the cats.

Tacoma had a moniker it had hoped would fade, "Kidnap Capital of the West." In 1935, three years after the Lindbergh kidnapping, nine-year-old George Weyerhaeuser, son of Washington's timber baron, John Philip Weyerhaeuser, had been grabbed off a Tacoma street in broad daylight. His parents paid a $200,000 ransom, the boy was released unharmed, and an arrest was made within days. Then, two days after Christmas, 1936, a man had broken into the mansion of Tacoma physician William Mattson. The intruder picked up 10-year-old Charles and left a ransom note asking for $28,000. Dr. Mattson tried desperately to follow the kidnappers' directions through notices in a Seattle newspaper, but communication broke down. Two weeks later the boy's naked body was found on a snow-covered field 60 miles north in Everett. He had been tied up and carried around in the trunk of a car. He died from blows to the head. The Mattson murder was never solved.

Beverly was eight years old when Charles Mattson was kidnapped and killed, an irony not lost on adult Bev, because Ann was eight when she disappeared. Bev and her friends would ride their bikes past the Mattson house. She would point to it and say, "That's where the boy was taken from."

On the night before Ann disappeared, her friend Susie had dinner at the Burrs'. Ann had two invitations to sleepovers, but Bev said no because school was starting soon.

At 8:30 p.m., the family's bedtime routine began. Greg and Julie, who was seven, went to the basement to spend the night in a fort they had made. Ann had a fungus under a fingernail, so Bev put mercurochrome on it and sent her and her three-year-old sister, Mary, upstairs to bed. Mary had broken her arm on a playground slide and was restless because of the cast on her arm.

Julie was just 14 months younger than Ann, and the girls shared a room. But because Julie was in the basement with Greg and Mary slept across the hall, Ann was alone. She took off her blouse, pedal pushers, and headband and put on the light blue nightgown with the blue and white flowers that Bev had sewn for her. Her doll, Tammy, wore an identical one. Ann never took off the necklace with the images of Jesus and Mary that she had received at her first Holy Communion in May. She also wore a bracelet that had her name, address, and phone number on it, just in case. The other side was engraved: Saint Christopher Protect Us.

Bev was exhausted from the warm weather and hadn't been sleeping well. For a couple of weeks, both Bev and Don had imagined they heard noises in the yard at night. At about 11 p.m. they locked up. Don put Barney, Ann's coal-black cocker spaniel, on the landing between the kitchen and the back door, and Bev put the chain lock on the front door. A living room window was open a couple of inches, so the wires to the TV antenna on the roof could snake through. It was a new TV, and Don hadn't found a way yet to accommodate the wires and also keep the window locked.

Late that night, Ann took Mary to their parents' room. Mary was crying because her cast was itching. Bev said a few reassuring words and told Ann to take Mary back upstairs.

Finally, the family was asleep. Barney raised a fuss during the night, but they assumed he was barking at the wind. The next afternoon, the front page of the newspaper had a story about the storm. It had rained half an inch and hundreds of people had lost power.

There was also a story about a girl who was missing.

1

Teddy

He carefully placed the knives around the sleeping girl, with the sharp, pointed ends closest to her neck and cheek. He didn't rush. He was capable of being quiet and patient; he wanted to get it just right.

And then he giggled. His 15-year-old aunt, Julia, awoke, more than a little frightened to find little Teddy lifting the covers and placing butcher knives beside her. Teddy was clearly delighted to have scared her.

When Julia gathered the knives and took them back down to the kitchen, she told her mother about the incident. But no one else in the family thought it was strange. It came back to her years later, after Ted became a suspect in several kidnappings and murders.

The child who would grow up to be a killer of such magnitude that law enforcement had to invent a term for his kind of terror—serial killer—was only three years old, but already he knew the business end of a knife.

Later, knives would not be his weapon of choice; instead, he would use his charisma, and tire irons, a crowbar, wooden clubs, a cleaver, panty hose, an ice pick, a hatchet, a lug wrench, a meat tenderizer, a metal bed frame, handcuffs, and his teeth. But at age three, you work with what you've got.

In 1946, when Eleanor Louise Cowell found herself unmarried and pregnant, she traveled to the Elizabeth Lund Home for Unwed Mothers in Burlington, Vermont. Since 1893, girls in the East had gone to stay at what was first known as the Home for Friendless Women. Louise (still known as Eleanor, until she moved west four years later) must have felt friendless. She was smart and popular in high school, but stayed close to home. She worked as a clerk at an insurance company near Philadelphia and lived in the family home with her parents, Samuel and Eleanor Cowell, and her two younger sisters. Samuel was a landscaper who owned a nursery in Roxborough, a community in northwest Philadelphia. Louise's mother was a "shadowy figure," dominated by her husband, suffering from depression and agoraphobia, and institutionalized more than once for shock treatments. She was ill much of her life and wasn't able to protect her eldest daughter when Louise needed it.

When Louise was 21 or 22, a coworker introduced her to a man who said he was a veteran of World War II and a graduate of the University of Pennsylvania. He implied there was family money. His name was Jack Worthington. The couple dated briefly, then Jack stopped calling. When she learned she was pregnant, Louise and her family's minister tried to find Jack Worthington. It was a dead end;

Jack Worthington had never attended the University of Pennsylvania, and he didn't have the well-paying job he said he had. He either vanished, or hadn't existed. That is the story that was told for years. There was a rumor that the father of Louise's baby was really an older, married member of her church. And there was a more sinister explanation for her pregnancy; maybe the reason why her father never "took off" after Jack Worthington, why he insisted on bringing the baby back to Philadelphia, and why Louise remained ambivalent even late in her life about keeping the boy, was that Samuel Cowell was the father. Louise is the only one who knows who Ted's father was, and beyond her tale of the mysterious Jack Worthington, she has never told.

Author Ann Rule, who knew Ted from his college years to the end of his life, always doubted the story of the vanishing birth father. "She never had a boyfriend, and suddenly she is pregnant?" Rule asked skeptically. She believes Ted's grandfather was his father, and that's why the baby was left at the Lund Home for Unwed Mothers in Vermont for his first few months. "The first woman in his life had lied and betrayed him," Rule said of the sense of abandonment Ted would experience his whole life.

The Cowell family was good at pretending problems didn't exist, but it was hard to hide Louise's pregnancy. She was president of the young people's group at her church until word got around that she was pregnant; then she was asked not to attend. As her pregnancy advanced, and her mother was too ill to accompany her to Burlington and her sister too young, the minister's wife made the journey with her. Two months later, on November 24, 1946, Louise gave birth to Theodore Robert Cowell. He weighed seven pounds, nine ounces, and the most his mother ever said about his birth was "there were no complications."

She went home alone, leaving her baby son with no mother to bond with, which child-development experts say is critical in the first few months of life. It was her father who insisted they retrieve him. Polly Nelson, a pro bono attorney who worked for three years to halt Ted Bundy's execution, believes Ted's mother had made her decision when she left Vermont and that she never intended to keep Ted. Her father was "stern and scary. He insisted Louise not put Ted up for adoption," Nelson said. "Three months alone in an orphanage; that's about as traumatic as it gets. Louise always seemed ambivalent. My impression is she never changed her mind about putting him up for adoption." Early in 1947, Louise returned to Vermont and collected the baby. They called him Teddy.

It was his first abandonment. Ted Bundy, who would have three names by the age of five, who would never know who his father was, who likely saw his beloved grandfather swing cats, kick dogs, and rage at his wife and daughters, would for his relatively short life feel a loneliness and a void that couldn't be filled. Until he learned he could fill it by bludgeoning, raping, strangling, biting, and beheading young women.

When it came to the story of Ted's conception, the family was secretive. His grandparents told some people—even family—that they had adopted a baby, but Teddy's great-aunt Virginia Bristol was skeptical. "When I heard Louise was 'not home' I knew things were not right. Next thing I heard was that Sam and Eleanor had adopted a boy," Bristol remembered years later. "I was smart enough to know damn well they weren't adopting this baby. No adoption agency would've given them one; Eleanor wasn't well enough to take care of one! I knew it had to be Louise's baby. But they wanted to cover up. All we ever got was evasions. I had a very secretive brother."

Others in the family were also skeptical of the "Jack Worthington" story but didn't dare discuss it; Samuel Cowell flew into a violent rage whenever the subject of Ted's paternity came up.

Ted told many versions of his parentage. He told some people that for years he believed his grandparents were his birth parents, and that Louise was his sister. At other times he said he always knew she was his mother. After Ted was arrested for murder, one of his teachers at Woodrow Wilson High School said that when Ted found out he was illegitimate, he "snapped." When he was in college he told a friend that it wasn't until a cousin teased him that he learned he was illegitimate.

He sobbed when he told a girlfriend what he knew of his birth, and he could appear resentful and ashamed of his mother. But other times he seemed to accept his illegitimacy with benign curiosity.

Whether he was the product of incest, or a brief tryst with Jack Worthington or a family friend, could Ted's rage at his mother and exposure to violent and disturbing behavior under his grandparents' roof explain why Ted Bundy could commit such atrocious crimes against young women?

The stories related by Louise's sisters and her aunts and uncles—Samuel's own daughters and siblings—have a gothic quality. Samuel had a stash of pornography that the very young Teddy must have seen, perhaps the kind that featured bondage and murder; Samuel was cruel to animals; Samuel raged at his employees; Samuel was a bully. Samuel's own brothers feared him and wished him dead; Samuel was "an extremely violent and frightening individual."

The youngest daughter described her father as a tyrant. Julia was just 12 years old when Louise came home with the baby (in a few years, Julia would be the teenager Teddy loved to scare with knives). She said that her father was so angry when she overslept one morning, and she was so afraid of him, that when he pulled her out of bed she stumbled and fell down a short flight of stairs. Samuel's sister said she always thought her brother was "crazy." Maybe young Teddy was the only person in Samuel Cowell's household who was *not* subjected to his verbal and physical abuse. Ted had only pleasant memories of those years, but it's not uncommon for adults, especially killers, to repress early memories of abuse, whether witnessed or experienced.

Ted told his longtime college girlfriend that he was disciplined harshly as a child but told others it amounted to nothing more than spanking. He also told the girlfriend that he avoided the draft during the Vietnam War because he had broken an ankle "when he was back east" and it had never healed right. "Back east" was his first four years, living at his grandfather's. Ted said he worshipped his grandfather, but he told a psychiatrist that Samuel Cowell was a bigot who hated blacks, Italians, Catholics, and Jews. Ted confirmed that his grandfather tortured animals and kept a large collection of pornography in his greenhouse.

Julia described her older sister Louise as being much like their father—temperamental, secretive, and undemonstrative. The family was good at denial. Louise remained adamant that her son could not be guilty of killing dozens of women. After he was executed, she continued to refer to his crimes as "those things" or "those terrible things."

Louise shrugged off questions about her father's abusiveness and what Teddy may have witnessed. It was only near the end of Ted's life that his mother revealed one family secret. Polly Nelson and psychiatrist Dr. Dorothy Otnow Lewis were trying to stop Ted's execution; they believed that he had sabotaged his trials and that abuse he either experienced or witnessed as a child should have been part of his defense. But Ted and his mother were not forthcoming about his childhood—until it was too late. As Nelson wrote, "Ted's mother, Louise, thinking that it was really her final chance to say something that could save Ted, called me at the hotel to admit that her father had been violent and probably had beat her mother. It was clearly a very, very difficult thing for her to say."

Dr. Lewis was not surprised. It confirmed what she knew about the childhoods of serial killers: their families would rather their loved ones die than reveal ugly secrets that might save them from the electric chair.

A professor of psychiatry at Yale and New York University, Dr. Lewis was studying juveniles on death row in the maximum-security Florida prison where Ted was housed. His attorneys asked if she would evaluate him. She says Ted told her about his "terrible depressions." She concluded that he fit other criteria she had formulated about people who murder. "Killers—not just serial killers—have been hideously abused as children," Dr. Lewis said. "What we have found is early, ongoing abuse, and a combination of other factors, including brain damage. Neurologists were saying there is no relationship [between brain damage and violence] but there is." Lewis's critics say she is sympathetic to killers. But the theory she was documenting in the 1980s—that serial killers show signs of childhood abuse, mental illness (in Ted's case, bipolar disorder), and brain damage—has gained credibility. The brains of killers are different from those of average adults.

Whatever the cause, Ted had been damaged emotionally. After a series of tests were performed on Ted in 1986, in preparation for another legal appeal, a psychologist concluded that Ted lacked "any core experience of care and nurturance or early emotional sustenance. Severe rejection experiences have seriously warped his personality development and led to deep denial or repression of any basic needs for affection. Severe early deprivation has led to a poor ability to relate to or understand other people."

We learn attachment from our mothers, and the cruelest deprivation is when we don't learn how to bond with others. Factors which cause a separation from a mother—including an unwanted pregnancy, being given up for adoption, or physical, emotional, or sexual abuse—lessen a child's sense of security. Children who become adults with attachment disorder have difficulty forming lasting relationships and never learn to trust.

Dr. Lewis calls the incident of three-year-old Teddy putting the knives beside his teenage aunt "extraordinarily bizarre behavior" for a toddler. "It's the kind of behavior that, to the best of my knowledge, you only see in youngsters who have themselves been seriously traumatized, who have either themselves been the victims of extraordinary abuse, or who have witnessed extreme violence among family members," she said.

Some of Ted Bundy's final words were about his childhood and his interest in the macabre. During his last hours he asked to see Dr. Lewis. He told her of how "very, very early" he had been fascinated with murder.

It might have been the incident with the knives. *Something* was the proverbial last straw as far as life at Teddy's grandparents' house. Something scared Louise's sisters and her aunt. Ted's great-aunt Virginia paid to send Louise and Teddy to the home of another brother, in Tacoma, probably to protect them, but from whom or what? Virginia explained it this way: "We felt Louise had to be rescued." Although she was moving thousands of miles away, Louise decided to drop her first name, Eleanor, and be known by her middle name, Louise. She also changed her last name and Teddy's to Nelson to pass herself off as a widow or divorcee.

But the move west came too late. Whatever had shaped Teddy had left its mark. Teddy was missing something, and it was more than a father, a mother who wanted him, or a home without mental illness and violence. He was missing empathy. He was missing an ability to form emotional bonds. He was missing a conscience.

2

Thursday, August 31

ANN WAS GONE.

It was early morning, about 5:15 a.m., and Beverly Burr had startled a neighbor by knocking on the front door.

Bev was in her bathrobe, and, as would often happen, she had forgotten she had bobby pins in her hair. She had awakened a few minutes before, checked on her children, and found Ann missing, the front door standing open, and the living room window open wider than usual. She hurried outside and searched the yard. As she walked around the house, she saw that a garden bench—the one she had stolen from an Indian reservation during a summer trip—had been moved from the back of the house near the garage to underneath the window on the west side of the house. That's when Bev began knocking on doors.

Some people tried to get Bev to come inside. Although it would be another warm day, it had just stopped raining, and the ground was wet. Oblivious to the dampness, Bev anxiously kept saying, "Ann is gone. Have you seen Ann?" They all said no, Ann wasn't there. Bev peered around them to see for herself.

Two houses east, Alice Bruzas was getting into her car. Many mornings Alice drove her eldest son, William, to his job as a psychiatric aide at the veteran's hospital. Alice's teenagers—13-year-old Frannie and 15-year-old Robert— were friendly with Ann.

Alice paused, letting Bev tell the story about Ann being missing, and then went upstairs and woke Frannie to see if she knew where Ann was. Frannie didn't. Although Frannie was five years older than Ann, they were occasional playmates. Frannie was too old for the dolls that Ann liked, but both girls had canaries and would get together at one house or the other to play with their birds. The families belonged to the same Catholic parish.

Alice seemed unconcerned about Ann being missing, and she hurried Bev away. Robert and Frannie thought of their mother as naively optimistic; she always, always, thought Ann would be found.

According to the police report, the first call to the Tacoma Police Department was made by Mrs. Donald B. Burr at 5:30 a.m. The dispatcher wrote that Ann Burr, age eight-and-a-half, had "taken off" in her night clothes.

Bev woke up Don and said she couldn't find Ann. They dressed quickly. Within a few minutes, two Tacoma police officers were at their door. Roland Otis, 25 years old, had been on the Tacoma police force three years and was assigned to juvenile cases. Like many of the men in the department, Otis grew up in Tacoma's north end.

It had been a busy evening for Otis and his partner, Leroy Bush. During the storm, they had come across the cause of the power outage. After a long dry spell, the heavy rain had knocked down a pole that snapped a power line at South 25th and Hosmer Street and started a fire. After reporting the fire to City Light crews, the policemen were ending their shift when they were dispatched to follow up on a report of a missing girl from 3009 North 14th Street.

As the rookie officers entered, they took a quick look around the house. The dining room was on the immediate right and the living room—the room with the window kept ajar for the TV antenna—on the left, the western most end of the house. To the rear of the dining room was a kitchen and breakfast nook. Bev and Don's bedroom was at the back on the main floor. A carpeted stairway in the center of the house led to the children's rooms on the second floor. Ann and Julie shared the front bedroom above the dining room. Mary's room was across the hall, and Greg's was above his parents' room. There was a spare room across from Greg's.

Bev told the police that Julie and Greg had slept in the basement the night before, how Mary and Ann had been up at least once in the middle of the night, and how she had found the window raised and the front door standing open, unlocked from the inside. The Burrs always locked the door at night, and the safety chain was always set. Bev and Don slept with their bedroom door open in case the children needed them.

The parents were worried. Officers Otis and Bush called the station to let the higher-ups know there was no trace of the girl. "This may not be just a missing girl," one of them told headquarters. As soon as more police officers arrived, Otis and Bush were sent to search the neighborhood. Among the residents they stopped to speak to was Yvonne Doherty, the mother of seven children. She was hanging wet laundry on the clothesline in the yard of her house, at 15th and Prospect, when the patrol car stopped. "They asked if I had seen a young girl," Doherty remembered. "I hadn't, and then I heard about it on the news." She would become one of Bev's closest acquaintances.

The officers drove and drove, looking for a small, golden-haired girl in a blue and white flowered nightgown.

Other police officers began going door to door, waking neighbors and asking if they had seen Ann or anyone in the neighborhood who "didn't belong" there. They asked permission to enter the homes and search from attic to basement.

Don got into one of the patrol cars, and he and the officer drove around the University of Puget Sound campus, a popular playground of children in the neighborhood. They didn't see Ann, but for the rest of his life Don would remember a young man he saw at one end of a deep pit. It was still too early for a crew to be at the excavation site, but the young man—he might have been a teenager— was stamping his feet in the dirt which the rain had turned to mud. He looked right at Don.

It was 6:45 a.m. when detectives Tony Zatkovich and Ted Strand arrived. The two men were handsome in a Hollywood B movie kind of way. Zatkovich looked like a boxer, with a square jaw and a nose that had gone a few rounds. Strand was dapper, with prematurely-gray hair and glasses. Bev thought he looked like a "courtly gentleman." The pair was famous for being members of Tacoma's vigilante police, a group of officers who in the 1940s went outside the police department to clean up corruption in the city. That's when Tacoma was known as "Seattle's dirty back yard," a "dirty city with dirty politics."

Zatkovich and Strand's white, 1958 Chevy four-door had an Oregon license plate, so they wouldn't look quite so much like cops. They didn't fool many people. Zatkovich's son, Dick, called them "Dick Tracy One and Dick Tracy Two." They didn't need to work at the "good cop, bad cop" routine. It came to them naturally. When questioning a suspect, Zatkovich would be the tough guy, and then leave the room in disgust; Strand would stay and befriend the suspect. But by the 1960s, the men missed the old days, when, as Zatkovich lamented, they "could kick a juvenile in the ass and send him home" with no parental or legal intervention.

Bev shared with the detectives the story that she would tell hundreds of times—how Ann brought

Mary to their room, how Bev had told Ann to "take her back up, dear." The detectives noted that Bev sometimes deviated about what time she had last seen the girls.

What Beverly didn't say—to the police, Don, or anyone—was that she had little hope. "When I first saw that window open, I knew I would never see her again. I knew I would never know what happened," she remembered years later. "It came to me, just like that. It was a strong feeling. When they were searching, I thought, 'What's the point?' I knew she was gone, and we would never see her again." Frightened and not daring to admit her feelings, Bev mostly sat and listened. Every time the phone rang she jumped, certain that Ann's body had been found.

The police tried speaking with Mary, who was the last to see Ann, but the three-year-old didn't remember if she had seen someone come upstairs during the night and take Ann away. They may have tried hypnosis, but Mary was too young to articulate if she had seen anything.

Then the police sat down with the other children. Julie, who was seven, told them of a person who had talked to her the day before. She didn't know if it was a man or woman because the person was dressed oddly, in a dark heavy coat, much too hot for a warm summer day. Bev remembered her children describing someone "dressed strangely in woman's [*sic*] clothes with a veil, someone Julie said looked just like a boy."

"Ann and I were playing on the porch with our Barbies," Julie said. "Mom was there, but when the phone rang, she went inside to answer it. The person in the coat came over and said, 'What house do you live in?' I said, 'This one.' They ran down the street, got in a waiting car, and drove off. I always felt a little guilty. I always thought I was the one who was supposed to be kidnapped."

The police took photographs inside and outside. They photographed Ann's unmade bed, with its bedspread of pink and turquoise flowers; Julie's was an exact twin. A stuffed monkey leaned against the wall, and a reading lamp balanced on Ann's headboard. Books were scattered on the floor. Ann excelled in all subjects at school, but especially art and reading. The police asked to borrow Tammy, the doll that eerily looked like Ann, with a matching nightgown. They needed Ann's fingerprints, and they wanted a good look at the fabric. Eventually police returned the doll to Bev. The powder used to lift fingerprints never disappeared.

Bev told the police that she and Don had heard Barney, their cocker spaniel, bark during the night, but they assumed he was alarmed by the sound of the wind and rain. The parents also told the police they thought they had heard someone in their yard a few nights before. Three neighbors, in fact, told police they had seen a Peeping Tom at their windows, but they couldn't describe the person.

There was little evidence. Police found a red thread snagged on the brick under the window. The bench that the intruder had moved under the window was taken to police headquarters for examination; police thought it had a footprint on it, maybe from a tennis shoe, about the size of a teenager's or a small man's foot. A thorough search of the yard also turned up a shoe print in the flower bed by the basement door, according to the police report, "as though someone had peered or tried to gain access to the basement." They made a mold of it. There were a few blades of grass on the living room floor. But what was a clue, and what was everyday life, tracked into the house by four rambunctious children, two adults, and a dog?

The police were disappointed. There was no sign of a struggle, nothing left behind. Did that mean that Ann knew whoever had entered the house? Had she encountered the man—from the beginning, the kidnapper was always assumed to have been a man—in the living room, before or after she had taken Mary to her parents' room? Was it someone who knew the layout of the house, and went directly to Ann's room? Or did she see someone she knew lean through the window and ask her to open the front door, and when she did, she was grabbed by him? Did she surprise a burglar? Why didn't she make any noise? Or did she? The police asked for a recent photograph of Ann, and Bev gave them the one of Ann wearing her lei.

At first, Bev and Don tried to shield their children from the news that Ann was missing. But Julie knew. "We either were told, or we knew it. I remember my mom pulling open all the kitchen drawers and looking under the sink. I thought she was looking for Ann. Of course, she was hysterical."

The two detectives tried to get a feeling about the parents. Don admitted he was sometimes firm with the children (he was firm with Bev, too) but said he hadn't spanked Ann in two years. He said he could not believe that Ann would be outside in the storm in a nightgown unless it was against her wishes. He described how Ann confided in Bev, how close mother and daughter were. Bev told the detectives that their lives centered on the children, that "they do not spend time gadding about."

It would have been hard for Bev to gad about. Because of Don, she didn't drive, didn't work, didn't have a barbecue in the backyard or Christmas lights on the front of the house, and had to quit volunteering at the League of Women Voters. She would find an interest, and Don would say "enough." She had thought of leaving him, but with Ann missing, that opportunity passed; she would need to focus on the other children to help them through the disappearance of their sister and to have the childhood they deserved. Until, or if, Ann came home, Bev still had three other young children.

Don was antsy and joined a group of searchers made up of police and volunteers. Within hours there would be hundreds of National Guardsmen scouring fields, abandoned buildings, gulches, sewers, garbage cans, and Tacoma's many waterways. At the same time, police were going one square block at a time, searching every house where someone was home to let them in. They combed every garage, shed, yard, garden, shrub, and hedge, including the area known as Buckley Gulch, an area close to the railroad tracks, and Commencement Bay. And then there were the roads that led to dead ends, to sites of trysts—both wanted and unwanted—that the police called "rape stations" and "petting grounds."

Just after noon on Thursday, detectives Zatkovich and Strand went to see Bev's mother, Marie Leach. She lived on the top floor of 31 Broadway, one of Tacoma's grand apartment buildings dating back to 1928. Marie had spent her married life living above or behind small grocery stores, so she enjoyed life at 31 Broadway. Although it was in the Stadium district, two miles from the Burr house, Marie's apartment was a straight shot east. Ann had said on several occasions that she thought she could find her own way to her grandmother's.

Marie and Bev weren't close. Marie's first child, Roy Leach Jr., called Buddy, had died of scarlet fever at age 10. The couple was devastated. Roy Sr. wore a black tie every day for the rest of his life in memory of his young son. They tried for another boy, but they had Bev. They tried again, and a few years later they finally had Jerry. But neither child would fill the void created by Buddy's death. Bev thought her mother was vain and that she underestimated Bev's mind and creative talents. Bev had defied her parents in the only ways she knew. As a child, her mother wanted Bev to study tap dancing; Bev refused to be Tacoma's answer to Shirley Temple and abruptly walked out of the class one day. As a teenager, Bev smoked because she thought Ingrid Bergman looked sophisticated in her movies with a cigarette in one hand. Bev's father wanted her to work in his grocery stores; instead, by age 15 she was selling floor lamps at Sears. Management was so impressed with the teenager that they suggested a career at the department store. "I thought about staying, but I was going to be a famous writer," Bev explained.

Then there was Don. Marie didn't think he was handsome. He hadn't finished college like Bev, who had even taught school briefly. Marie thought Don was too blue collar; he was a civilian employee at Camp Murray, the Washington State National Guard base. In acknowledgement of his status, Don called himself "just a lunch bucket."

It's not that Bev celebrated when her mother died at age 95, but she enjoyed telling the story of how Marie slipped on ice cream on her kitchen floor, and lay there alone for a day until a neighbor found her. Marie never really recovered and died a short while later.

The police noted that Ann's grandmother "did not seem excited, and seemed to think that Ann was somewhere in the neighborhood, sleeping. She says they are a very close family, go to church every Sunday together, but did say that of the four children, Ann is known to be a little irrational." The detectives asked Marie about any bad blood in the family. She told them about the rift that had formed between Don's family and hers. Bev and Don had been married by a justice of the peace on August 6, 1951. But Bev was Catholic, and she thought if the family was more involved in parish life at St. Patrick's, it might help smooth out some rough spots in her marriage. In the spring of 1961, about the time Ann was confirmed, Don agreed to take instruction. The couple remarried, this time in the Catholic Church. Although he never formally joined the church, Don's parents were furious and talked of disowning him.

Don and his father had also argued bitterly over the sale of the logging operation they ran in California in the early 1950s. Don's father sold the business without telling him. The men had heated arguments about it. His father gave him $26,000 as his part of the sale, and another $8,000 to buy a house. Don didn't think the payment reflected his fair share of the business.

By 2 p.m., nine hours after Ann went missing, the police had assembled a list of what the department called "known sex perverts, child molesters, exhibitionists, sex odd balls, and weirdos," a list that would grow into the hundreds in just days. The detectives systematically began interviewing each one. There were dozens of reports during the day that raised the hopes of police. Some were about old incidents. A salesman had attempted to force his way into the home of Mrs. F__ about a year before, but left when she said her husband was home. There were dozens of stories about Peeping Toms, unknown cars in the neighborhood, and a teenage boy opening and closing a large, long-bladed knife as he paced the sidewalk. People called to report the odor of decaying flesh and mounds of dirt that seemed to have appeared overnight. When they dug, police found a decomposed cat or a calf that had died at birth.

Officers R. Baldassin and J. Vejvoda were assigned to interview Ann's friends, Christine K__ and Susan E__. Both had played with Ann the day before. Susie had been at the Burrs' for dinner, and then the girls went to Susie's home. She told police that Ann didn't seem any different than usual. The officers wrote, "Ann didn't say anything about running away, or any trouble she was having." Ann was invited to stay with Susie at the girl's grandmother's house, but called later to say that "something came up," and she couldn't go. The police asked Susie's mother to talk to her daughter in private to determine if 15-year-old Robert Bruzas, the boy who flirted with Ann, had ever been inappropriate with the girls. Mrs. E__ spoke alone with her daughter and reported back that Robert had never taken advantage of the girls in any way.

Christine told them about the neighborhood nudist. Christine said that Mr. D__ was very friendly with the small children in the neighborhood. They went to his yard to pick plums from his tree, and he gave them candy. She said that on occasion Mr. D__ kissed their hands and put his arm around them. He patted their buttocks, too. Christine's mother said she often had seen Mr. D__ walking in the neighborhood at about five o'clock in the morning. And she said he visited her when she was pregnant, bringing her a rose each day. On these visits Mr. D__ made comments such as "I like to see women pregnant," and, "I think pregnant women are beautiful." Other neighbors talked of seeing Mr. D__ nude in his yard.

Detectives Zatkovich and Strand were frank with Bev and Don: maybe Ann hadn't cried because she willingly left her home with someone she knew. Could it have been a neighbor? A relative? A family friend? The Burrs began to make a list of names the police should check out.

The conversation kept coming back to Robert. They learned from Bev that Robert didn't seem to have any friends of his own age. Bev told the detectives, "He spends time playing with kids out on his front lawn, but they are all younger. He is such a nice boy. He spent a lot of time watching Don build a patio floor in the back. And he told me that he thinks Ann is quite a girl, or his girl, or words to that effect." Zatkovich and Strand made a note to talk to the teenager.

Bev admitted to the police that Ann may have known children or even teenagers in the neighborhood that she wasn't aware of. If Robert flirted with her, maybe other boys did too as they passed by on their bicycles, on their way to paper routes or Boy Scout meetings.

Bev also mentioned Leonard A__, the piano teacher Ann had studied with for two years. Ann had a lesson every Tuesday, at 3:30 p.m. Just two days before she vanished, she had completed Book 1 of the *Eric Steiner Piano Course.* She was allowed to walk by herself the four blocks to Mr. A's__ house on North Puget Sound Avenue. This was just one example of how relatives thought Ann was given far too much independence. She had been walking several blocks alone since the second day of kindergarten.

The police had no record of Mr. A__ ever being in trouble. When they went to his house he showed detectives his studio in his basement. He did admit to "disciplining" Ann a time or two. This would have puzzled Bev if she had heard his remark because Ann loved to play the piano, loved to practice, and was always prepared for her lesson. What could she have done that warranted "disciplining"?

As afternoon became evening, the police installed a phone recording system in the Burrs' basement. It would record all calls, including the ransom demands police assumed would come. The most famous kidnappings in Tacoma history had not been random—they had been for ransom. There was just one problem. Unlike the families of the Weyerhaeuser and Mattson boys, Bev and Don Burr didn't have any money.

3

Evening, August 31

STRANGERS—AND DON'S SIDE OF THE FAMILY—thought Bev and Don had money. They didn't, but Bev's mother, Marie Leach, did. Nearly 50 years later, Bev would share a secret that not even her own children knew. Her father, born Roy Gleitz, had come west from St. Louis at a young age, changing his name to Leach. He first worked in a haberdashery in Seattle, but wanted to be his own boss. He moved to Tacoma and opened a small grocery store, building loyalty with his customers by keeping the store open seven days a week until 11 p.m. every night, even after he had crippling rheumatism. Bev's father pretended to look the other way when the monsignor for the Seattle archdiocese, which included Tacoma, walked out the door without paying for boxes of donuts. Every day Roy Leach wore slippers with holes, but when he died in 1956, he was worth a million dollars.

So there was some truth to the rumor that Bev and Don had access to money. If they needed to, they could offer a ransom, but only with Marie's help.

There *was* a Donald Burr in Tacoma who presumably had more money than Bev and Don, and he also had a nine-year-old daughter. Could she have been the intended kidnap victim? Donald F. Burr was an architect and lived in nearby Lakewood. Detectives Smith and Seymour contacted him just hours after Ann disappeared and met him at his office on Mt. Tacoma Drive SW. This Don Burr told the police the complicated story of the previous 10 years of his life. Originally from South Dakota, he had served in the Army in Europe during the war. In Austria he met a girl, Lepoldianna, nicknamed Poldi. They married, and he brought Poldi to America in 1947. Two years later, the Army recalled him and sent him to Korea. He was injured and spent a year at Madigan Army Medical Center in Tacoma, the same hospital where Johnnie Bundy, stepfather to a young boy named Teddy, was working as a cook. In May 1952, less than seven months before Ann Burr was born, Donald and Poldi's daughter, Debra Sue, was born. When the girl was only six weeks old, Poldi insisted on returning alone to Austria for a vacation.

Young Debra Sue was taken to South Dakota to stay with her paternal grandparents. Poldi returned after three months. Her husband learned that she had met an older man on her way to Europe. Poldi lasted a week back in Tacoma, then fled to Chicago where her new lover, Emile Holliner, worked at the Blackstone Hotel, which was a fixture in local and national politics, best-known as the source of the phrase "smoke-filled room."

Donald and Poldi sued each other for divorce, and he won custody of Debra Sue. Poldi never again tried for custody, and she had visited her daughter only two or three times since her birth. Donald F. Burr eventually married a widow, adopted her two children, retrieved Debra from South Dakota, and fathered two more children. There was lingering animosity because Poldi would not give the new Mrs. Burr permission to adopt Debra.

Debra did not know that the woman with the odd accent who sent her a $25 savings bond every year on her birthday was her mother. Donald told the detectives he planned to wait until Debra was older to tell her how her mother had deserted them.

The detectives were, of course, curious: would Poldi attempt to get Debra back by staging a kidnapping? Had she hired someone who had bungled things and taken the wrong girl, the daughter of the *other* Don Burr? A mother who had walked away from her daughter and taken the trouble to see her only a couple of times in nine years didn't sound like a woman desperate enough to plot a kidnapping. Even her old friends in Tacoma laughed at the idea. They said Poldi didn't care enough about her daughter to try to kidnap her. Donald told police he lived in an expensive home in the Tacoma suburb of Lakewood, and it could give the impression to a kidnapper that he had money. He was very concerned that his daughter might have been the intended victim. FBI agents in Chicago agreed to check out Poldi and Emile Holliner, who were now suspects in the disappearance of Ann Burr.

Donald F. Burr also told police about the numerous phone calls he received for the other family. One time the architect's wife answered the phone and heard a man say, "Mrs. Burr, that husband of yours is going to get himself killed. He is a matinee lover, and he better stay away from my wife." Then the caller hung up. Several other times women called and asked if Burr was going to "come down to the apartment."

Donald B. Burr (the one who referred to himself as "just a lunch bucket") did own some apartments. Bev had never liked Don's side business. Tenants were always coming and going, and he had to spend his weekends making endless repairs. Bev was always a little scared when Don would go to collect the rents.

Detectives P.P. Schultz and J. Fitzpatrick got a list of Don's former tenants, and decided to pay his current ones a visit. Those visited included Miss Ethel F__, an elderly woman, and Mrs. Georgia N__, who explained that her husband was in the county jail and on his way to the state penitentiary in Walla Walla to serve 20 years for "falsifying a report on food allotment program." There were a couple of vacancies, and one couple was on an extended vacation to Idaho. There were also a Latvian couple with a young son, and a man separated from his wife. The officers picked up a trustee from the city jail, gave him a large lamp, and had him crawl through a trap door, a cellar, and the attic. There was no sign of Ann.

All the tenants were concerned over the disappearance of Don's daughter and spoke highly of him. They did recall one incident, though. Don Burr had evicted "a colored family" after their son struck the son of the Latvian couple. Maybe there were some lingering bad feelings toward the landlord? When the detectives asked the elderly woman in apartment A about the episode, she barked that the boy who was slugged had it coming.

The police also wanted to check out people who had done odd jobs for Don, including a Negro (as African Americans were called in Tacoma in 1961, and sometimes even now) and his 21 or 22-year-old son who had done some painting at the apartment building shortly before Ann disappeared. Bev and Don found it odd that when the son came to their house to pick up his pay a few days later, he knew exactly which alley and driveway to turn into.

In her quest to try to help the police by giving them names of people to talk to, Bev told them of her suspicions of a neighbor she described as overly polite and insincere. The detectives wrote down the information, smiled to themselves, and dismissed her tip. They had more likely suspects to follow up with.

Bev, whose only dream was to be a novelist or a journalist, suddenly found her family on the front page of the newspaper. The early afternoon edition of the Tacoma News Tribune featured a small story. It said that eight-year-old Ann Marie Burr, daughter of Donald B. Burr and Beverly Burr, of 3009 North 14th Street, Tacoma, was found missing from her bed early that morning. “She is believed to be a possible victim of amnesia,” the story reported.

By the second edition, later that same afternoon, a huge headline on the front page proclaimed: “Girl, 8, Vanishes From Home—Chief Hager Calls For Wide Hunt,” accompanied by the photo the family had given police. In the picture, Ann, not usually demure, is standing alone, looking solemn, her hands together in front of her. She is wearing the paper lei, a headband, a blouse with short, puffy sleeves, and pedal pushers.

Det. Richardson talked to reporters about the parents. He said that Bev and Don had “held up well” until about noon from the strain of their worries. But as the hours passed without any word of Ann, there was increasing indication of apprehension. That may have been when seven-year-old Julie saw her mother hysterical, endlessly searching through kitchen drawers, as if she had misplaced Ann like a serving spoon.

Everyone in Tacoma wanted to hear from the parents. How was the mother coping after the disappearance of her child? Bev was almost always the parent quoted in articles. She sounded hopeful. “She may show up any minute,” Bev said. “She might have walked outside and got locked out some way. She knew her phone number. If only we would get a call.”

A gaunt and sad Bev Burr was interviewed by a Seattle television station, which had made a rare trip out of the city, with a huge camera and lights, to record the search on black and white film. "Probably the worst has happened to our little girl. And, uh, I just hope they find her," Bev told the reporter.

Bev would second-guess herself—and the police—for the rest of her life. "I should have let her stay with [a neighbor child] that night. Ann was so trusting. It was a big mistake. We taught her everyone was good. We didn't teach them that people could be bad." She had her doubts about the police, too. "I always thought they should have set up a roadblock, instead of asking questions, so many questions."

Police did not set up a roadblock, maybe because Tacoma had dozens of entrances and exits, by land, sea, and air. There was wilderness to both the east and west, and there was water, a lot of it. Tacoma is on Puget Sound, a body of water with a complex series of islands, inlets, and harbors bounded on the north by Canada and surrounded by two massive mountain ranges, the Olympics and the North Cascades. It would be easy to disappear with a small girl.

Julie, Greg, and Mary were sent to a neighbor's home for the day, so Bev and Don could speak candidly with police and so they could telephone family members.

Don's younger brother, Raleigh, and his wife Sharon, arrived from the small town of Grandview, in eastern Washington. Although Raleigh was 12 years younger than Don, they were close. Don,

Raleigh, and their sisters had grown up in Grants Pass, Oregon.

As a teenager, Raleigh had worked for Don and their father, logging in northern California. Raleigh had babysat Ann when she was a newborn while they all lived in tents in the summer. When Ann went missing, Raleigh had to borrow a car from the dealership where he worked to make the long, hot drive over the mountains to Tacoma.

"There was a lot of police activity," Raleigh Burr remembered about the day. "They questioned us—where we were from, who we were. There was coffee on the stove. Don was sitting on a couch with his eyes closed. I tried to talk to him, but he didn't respond. I didn't see any hysteria. Some people had brought food, probably Bev's church friends or high school friends. I was so sure everything would turn out all right; there must be an explanation." Other family arrived, too. Jeff Leach was Bev's nephew, her brother Jerry's boy. Jeff was exactly Ann's age. His family often joined the Burrs at Fox Island, where Bev's father owned two small, rustic cabins. After the phone call that Ann was missing, Jeff's family immediately left their home in Seattle for Tacoma. Jeff Leach remembers helping put up the posters with Ann's photo, and the tension and fear in the Burr house. "It terrified me a lot," he says of his cousin's disappearance. "We didn't wander too far."

After the citizens of Tacoma saw the newspaper stories about Ann Burr, they telephoned the police with tips. Sometimes the calls were about the obvious. Had the police checked the Burr's attic?

Were they *sure?* What about the furnace? Police got calls from a man with a divining rod, offering to help look for Ann. Another said that if he was given a sock of Ann's, he was sure he could trace her. The police considered them "crackpots" but politely took their names, phone numbers, and addresses and checked to see, first, if they were known sex offenders. Then they followed-up on some of the tips. One caller said Ann was in a Portland area hotel with two men and a woman. Tacoma police asked their colleagues in Portland to check it out. Within a surprisingly short period of time—a couple of hours—Portland police called back and claimed to have contacted dozens of hotels. They said they couldn't find any record of two men, a woman, and a child registered.

Other residents of Tacoma just appeared at the Burr house wanting to help search. The men found themselves subjected to questioning by police. Criminals, after all, were known to return to the scene of the crime and act like a Good Samaritan, offering to help. The men were taken to police headquarters, questioned about the unusual interest they were taking in the case, and released.

Many people in the Burr's North Tacoma neighborhood reported they had heard or seen prowlers or had found their flower gardens trampled; they could give no details but were usually cooperative when police knocked on their doors, asking to search their homes and basements. The exception was Mrs. S__ of North 13th Street.

"Widow, very old, would not let us search house," Officers Meyer and Burk wrote in their report.

They visited one neighbor, Dorothy H__, who had arrived home late the night before, the night of the storm, after taking inventory at her bar. As she was doing some wash in the basement, she heard a noise and saw the silhouette of a man's head very close to a kitchen window. She described him as a large person with bushy hair. She screamed and he ran. She called the police and reported the incident. The police log showed that she had called at 3:30 a.m. on Thursday, August 31, just two hours before Ann was found missing.

Wives called the police to report that their husbands were acting suspiciously and were spending a lot of time under their house for some unknown reason. Mothers gave alibis to unemployed sons who had a record of brushes with the law or had spent time in the insane asylum. Neighbors reported seeing a midget with a beard peeking in windows. Another neighbor regaled the police with stories of how he had first had sex at age six, and had impregnated one girl when he was just nine.

What police call "sightseer traffic" began. Hundreds of cars drove past the Burr house, slowing as if to look at Christmas decorations or the scene of a traffic accident. The address—printed in every story and every edition of the newspaper—was by now familiar. Just as Bev and her friends had bicycled by the Mattson home as children and never failed to remark on it being the site of a famous kidnapping, so strangers wanted to see for themselves where this one had happened and feel grateful it wasn't them.

In the late afternoon, Tacoma Police Chief Don Hager met with Elgin Olrogg of the Tacoma bureau of the FBI. Later, Agent Olrogg told reporters that he was only observing the case. Police Inspector Smith told reporters that "the girl's case has not yet been classed as a kidnaping [*sic*] as thus far there are no facts to support such a supposition."

The FBI observed for days, never putting its experience at kidnappings to use. It released statements explaining that there was no evidence that someone had entered the Burr house, and that it was convinced Ann had probably wandered or run away. Bev called that "absolutely stupid."

Detectives Zatkovich and Strand agreed. They had no use for the FBI. "We used to have to tell the FBI, 'You guys get out of our hair and we'll solve the case, and then we'll call you,'" Zatkovich once explained. "They would send two carloads of strangers over from Seattle on every bank robbery, and we had to wait until they got out of here to go to work."

A caption on a photograph of Ann published that week in the Tacoma News Tribune bluntly posed this question: "Was Ann Marie the victim of a sex pervert, or was she abducted by someone who wanted a child?" There was no caption or headline that could suggest anything that hadn't already occurred to Bev and Don. It was easy to imagine the worst.

Very quickly, the rumors began. Bev had been married before and the child's *real* father had grabbed Ann. Don used to go by another name when he was logging in California. The couple was hiding something. They weren't really the girl's parents. They had left their children alone, and see what happens? Bev overheard a woman in a restaurant say, "You know who killed her—the mother."

Bev and Don were hurt by the rumors. Plus, the police were stepping up their questioning of Don, asking him pointed questions. So Bev and Don talked it over, asked a relative to stay with the children, and appeared at the police station insisting they wanted to take polygraph tests. The police agreed. Bev was nervous; what if the results made them look suspicious? But the test showed that neither was involved in Ann's disappearance. Bev made sure the newspapers reported it.

Don couldn't just sit in the house and wait. He and Raleigh and their eldest brother Barney took a walk in the neighborhood. They were searching for Ann, of course. Raleigh was pleasantly startled when he heard a voice say, "Hi, Uncle Raleigh." He turned around excitedly. "I thought it was Ann, but it was Greg," he remembered. The three brothers walked up to the construction sites at the college. When they returned from their walk they made a suggestion to the police that was entered in that day's police report: "Mr. Burr and a couple of his relatives went for a walk this evening, and when they returned said there are several excavation holes in the UPC [*sic*] area which are full of water several feet deep. Possibly the Public Works Department can be contacted today to pump out those holes in case the missing girl could have fallen in." They were the same deep ditches where Don had seen the young man with the smirk that morning, kicking dirt back and forth with his foot as he watched the search for Ann. Many years later, when another Tacoma child became famous, Don was certain he recognized the face.

At 5:20 p.m. Don Burr answered the telephone and heard a young girl's voice say.

This is Ann Marie Burr ...

Don swore that's what he heard. But the police, who were nearby and monitoring the calls, were quite certain that the girl did not say her full name. They would never know for certain because the recording machine malfunctioned, and the call was not recorded. But Don believed it was his daughter's voice.

Eight minutes later the phone rang again. This time Det. Zatkovich answered it and a young girl's voice said.

This is Ann Marie...

There was a brief pause, and then the caller hung up. This call was not recorded either. Were they prank calls? Ann never referred to herself as Ann Marie. But maybe a kidnapper had ordered her to say her name, and he thought she was called 'Ann Marie.' Wouldn't a kidnapped child scream for their parent rather than recite their full name?

When the horrible day came to an end, Bev put the children to bed. It was just like the evening before, but nothing like the evening before. Don put Ann's cocker spaniel Barney on the landing. Detectives stayed in the basement in case the Burrs received a phone call from the kidnapper. Outside, unmarked police cars watched the house. They also watched the house of Mr. D__, the exhibitionist that the police thought liked children and pregnant women a little too much.

Detectives Zatkovich and Strand wrote in their report that night that... "...extensive questioning of the parents failed to shed any light on the girl's disappearance. Both of them claim that she is an intelligent girl, although quiet; that she has good habits, obeys her parents, goes to bed early, sleeps well; however, she does read occasionally in the evening in bed and, to their knowledge, she has no problem of walking in her sleep or anything of that nature."

And then, for the first of hundreds of evenings to come, Detectives Tony Zatkovich and Ted Strand sat in Tony's driveway in their white Chevy, the car they hoped wouldn't give them away as cops, lit cigarette after cigarette, and talked about how an eight-year-old girl could vanish. Zatkovich wasn't so sure about Don. He thought he was a little shady, an odd duck, stern. And there were those calls that were made to the wrong Burr house, threatening "the matinee lover." Strand agreed with his partner that the kidnapper must know Ann, must know the layout of the house, and must have coaxed her outside. At some point they made a bargain to quit smoking. Zatkovich did quit; Strand lasted a few days, then went back to his Camels.

The Burr house was filled with relatives staying the night. Julie, Greg, and Mary were confused and scared. Julie, just seven, was suddenly the eldest of the children, a responsibility that would weigh on her. Ann wasn't just Julie's older sister—she was her best friend.

"I remember being terrified to go upstairs to bed alone," Julie recalled, "and to get from there to the safety of the main floor where my parents were. I couldn't stay in the room Ann and I had shared for years, so I moved to an empty room on the other side of the house upstairs, and Mary moved into our room."

Bev tried to reassure her children. "They needed me very much, and I had to remember that. They were terrified. They asked, 'Will he come and get us, too?'"

4

Ted

TED HELD HIS NOSE. TACOMA STUNK. HE HAD always thought it stunk. He noticed it as soon as they arrived in the city, after his mother cruelly yanked him from his grandfather's house—the only home and the only father-figure he had known—and brought him to this city that smelled. The smell's origin was tidal flats, sulfur emissions from paper mills, and 100 years of chemicals dumped into Commencement Bay, creating one of the most polluted bodies of water in the country. The stink even had a name: the Tacoma Aroma. You tried to get out of its way when the wind was from the east.

Ted was embarrassed by his family's descent into working-class status and especially by the Nash Rambler his mother and step-father drove. Ted fantasized about being adopted by western actor Roy Rogers (*he* wouldn't drive a Nash Rambler). There would be money, and Ted would have his own horse.

The boy admired his great-uncle John Cowell, whom he and Louise stayed with when they first arrived in Tacoma. John Cowell was as different from his older brother, Samuel, as he could be (except they both married women named Eleanor, which was also their mother's name). Samuel, Ted's grandfather, was the oldest of seven children; John was the youngest. Twenty-three years and a world of differences separated them.

John Cowell was a music professor at the University of Puget Sound. While living in his home, Ted was introduced to the culture and status he longed for and thought he deserved. But he was just a temporary visitor and had to watch his cousin, a boy just a few months older than he was, thrive in the home Ted thought he should have. If Roy Rogers didn't adopt him, maybe his great-uncle could.

Cowell drove exotic European cars, which turned heads in Tacoma. After living and performing in Europe, he had a French Simca shipped home, and later he drove a Peugeot. "I know he was enamored of our family, he romanticized it," Ted's cousin Edna Cowell Martin said. There was a lot to romanticize. Her father wasn't just a music teacher; he was a noted composer and performer. He'd been a piano prodigy at age six, won a scholarship to The Juilliard School as a teenager, been a student of Aaron Copland's at Tanglewood, earned his graduate degree at the Yale School of Music, performed at Carnegie Hall, and was friends with Leonard Bernstein.

In addition to riding in a Simca and a Peugeot, Edna and her older brother John (the cousin Ted envied), went to private schools in Europe and Seattle. The Cowells had a beach house near Longbranch, on a peninsula west of Tacoma. Edna remembers the Bundy family arriving for a visit, all crowded into the Nash Rambler.

The Cowells were educated, well-traveled, and classy, but they weren't wealthy. When Louise and Teddy arrived in Tacoma in 1951, the Cowells were living in a modest house on Alder, just two blocks from 3009 North 14th, where Don and Bev Burr moved their growing family in 1955. By then, Ted and his mother, step-father, and Ted's young half-siblings were living on South Sheridan, still in North Tacoma. Later they moved to N. Skyline Drive, not far from the suspension bridge across Puget Sound connecting Tacoma to the Kitsap Peninsula. The Cowells, meanwhile, had moved to N. Puget Sound Avenue, still near the university, and Ted would ride his bicycle back and forth. Despite Ted's jealousy, he and his cousin John Jr. were good friends. But by the time he was a young teenager, Ted was spending a lot of time alone. He liked to roam on his bike. He liked alleys, and there were alleys everywhere in his former neighborhood in North Tacoma.

Ted felt his mother married beneath herself. She came from a family that produced a musician, a college president, and successful business owners. They were from the east, and while the east had more than its share of towns that smelled, Ted didn't remember them. Ted had always been proud of how his mother had excelled in high school, how involved she had been in school activities, and how well-liked she was. That was all before Jack Worthington or whatever his name was.

When Ted and his mother first arrived in Tacoma, Louise found an office job, and not long after she went to a church social at Tacoma's First Methodist Church, the same denomination that had asked her to leave the young adults group when her pregnancy came to its attention. But that was back in Pennsylvania, and now she had a new identity. It was never quite clear if this young woman was gamely raising her younger brother or a son whose father had died tragically in the war, or even worse, abandoned her. She was now Louise Nelson, and her son was Teddy Nelson.

At the church she met John Culpepper Bundy, called Johnnie, a soft-spoken Southerner who had been a cook on several large ships during World War II. He was from North Carolina, and one of 12 children. He was cooking at a military hospital near Tacoma when he met Louise. They married just a few months after meeting in 1951, and Louise soon gave birth to a girl, then a boy, then another girl, then another boy, and almost overnight Ted had not only lost his grandfather, he had lost his mother to Johnnie and to four young half-siblings. His tenuous and confusing connection to Louise became even more fragile. For a boy who felt deprived and abandoned, it was enough to make him mad. In the final hours of his life, he would express confusion over the anger he felt toward his mother.

From a young age, Ted was a snob. Johnnie wasn't good enough for his mother. Tacoma couldn't compare with the east coast, and it seemed to always lose out when compared with Seattle. It's often said that the distance between Seattle and Tacoma is a lot more than 30 miles. Of the two cities, Tacoma should have become the bigger and more prosperous. It was the Pacific terminus of the Northern Pacific Railroad beginning in 1873. Tacoma's Commencement Bay is a better harbor than Seattle's Elliott Bay. Tacoma had strong unions and, as Rudyard Kipling wrote while passing through in 1889, Tacoma was "literally staggering under a boom of the boomiest." A fire started by boiling glue at a cabinet-making shop had recently destroyed the entire downtown of Seattle, helping to level the playing field a little. Tacoma could, for once, lord its success with its port and logging over Seattle, which was now just "a horrible black smudge."

That changed again when gold was discovered along the Klondike River in Alaska, in 1896. Seattle became the "Gateway to the Gold Fields," the jumping off point for thousands of prospectors headed to the Yukon Territory. It was Seattle merchants who equipped them for their trip.

By the early 1960s, the city where Bev Burr had spent her entire life and where Ted Bundy was uprooted to, had started a long decline. Within a few years, the birthplace of Bing Crosby, the city where Frank and Ethel Mars stirred their chocolate, and where Nalley's perfected its pickles, would be characterized by its own mayor as looking "bombed out" like "downtown Beirut." As the journalist and historian Murray Morgan wrote, "Tacoma's struggle... had become not to surpass Seattle but to survive as something other than suburb or satellite to the metropolis, to remain a community with a distinct economic base and personality." One of the detective magazines put it a little less elegantly in a headline: "Beneath the snowcapped peak of Mount Rainier lies a boiling cesspool."

Instead of being adopted by his great-uncle, Teddy was adopted by Johnnie. Now the boy had the third name of his young life. But Ted and Johnnie never formed a strong bond. Ted's friends remember when he stopped calling Johnnie "Dad" and started to call him by his name, or not refer to him at all. Ted didn't want to be pals with Johnnie.

Ted was embarrassed that Johnnie, a diminutive man, had no higher aspirations than to spend his life as a cook at a military hospital. Johnnie was good-hearted and entertained people with stories about making "scrambled eggs for five hundred people and cars that broke down." In Ted's eyes, Johnnie was a redneck. But Ted was special. Ted skied. Ted was going to college.

As a child, Ted was capable of throwing tantrums; he admitted as an adult that it was probably because he was jealous about losing his mother to Johnnie. And there was anger close to the surface. Ted's elementary school report cards had As and Bs but a teacher's note pointed out that Ted needed help controlling his temper. In photos with his best friend Doug Holt and Doug's sister Sandi, Ted has clenched fists—even at his friend's birthday party. Sandi says Ted's hands often formed fists, and that he could sock another child, even his friends, with no warning.

From a young age, Ted liked to sneak out of the house. Because it got hot in the upstairs of their house, Sandi and Doug Holt spent every summer night in a tent in their backyard on North Howard Street, about a block from Ted's. Ted would appear and spend a few hours in the tent with them. He wouldn't sleep there, but the three would try and identify the constellations in the Tacoma sky, and the boys would discuss their latest game of "getting over." They liked to trick people, put something over on them, and of course, not get caught. There were incidents only his youngest childhood friends knew of. Sandi Holt, who as a child followed Ted and Doug everywhere, is convinced her father sexually molested Ted.

C__ Holt was a highly decorated World War II radio operator who flew dozens of combat missions. After the Army, he had a career at the Puget Sound Naval Shipyard in Bremerton, Washington. On a Boy Scout camping trip one summer, the other troop members—including Doug—caught Ted and C__ Holt undressed in the middle of the day in one of the tents. Maybe they were drying off after swimming, maybe not. But it was apparent that something had been going on—and it wasn't innocent. Doug believed that something definitely "kinky" had happened between his father and Ted, that the two were a little too "buddy-buddy." The other boys teased Ted; that may have been the outing when Ted hit a fellow Scout member over the head with a stick. The father of one of the other boys berated C__ Holt for being in the tent with Ted, but beyond that there were no repercussions for Holt. Ted abruptly stopped going on Boy Scout camping trips but wouldn't explain why.

Sandi and Doug were well aware of their father's ability to abuse children. He sexually molested them all of their childhood.

Ted was having trouble controlling his compulsion to "creep around in the darkness." Sandi says she saw Ted use his pocket knife to cut open animals, douse them with gasoline, and set them on fire. He and Doug also used knives to slash the leather seats in expensive cars in the neighborhood. Ted would try to "pants" young girls, luring them into the woods, pulling down their pants, and urinating on them. Doug Holt was a little smaller than Ted, but he hit his best friend when Ted tried to drag Sandi into the woods. Sandi Holt never forgot the dark look that could overtake Ted, how the color of his irises changed, how she could suddenly be scared of her brother's best friend.

Ted's early abuse of animals was textbook. He was imitating his grandfather, and it was a rehearsal for later violence, a way to practice before moving on to killing women. It also served as a release from his depression, a mood enhancement, and was a symptom of his attachment disorder. From childhood, Ted fit another psychological model: he had quantities of fearlessness and aggression, which are signs of a lack of empathy.

The North Skyline area was a neighborhood of modest homes and families with modest means surrounded by wealthier neighborhoods. According to Sandi Holt, Ted was jealous of his peers, the children of doctors and lawyers. His rage at someone or something was building. As a young teenager—when his friends were beginning to date—Ted was seeking out pornography and reading about gruesome crimes. "He was extremely lonely," attorney Polly Nelson explained. "He was wandering alone all the time, to stay out of the house, going through garbage cans looking for porn."

And he found some, whether it was in garbage cans, or, as he told his friend Jerry Bullat, right in plain sight on a Tacoma sidewalk. For six years, from seventh grade at Hunt Junior High School until they graduated from Wilson High School, class of '65, Ted sat behind Bullat in homeroom. Since they were thrown together alphabetically in class and in yearbooks, the two boys formed a friendship based on their shared love of skiing, especially night skiing at Snoqualmie Pass, 65 miles east of Tacoma.

One day, Ted took Bullat aside at school to show him a photo. It was old, it was black and white, and Bullat was shocked: it was a photo of a man and a woman having oral sex. Ted said he found it on the sidewalk, but Sandi Holt says Ted had discovered that her father—Ted's abuser—hid his porn outside, in a bag under grass clippings.

Bullat doesn't remember Ted ever mentioning the ankle that was broken as a child. It didn't seem to slow down his skiing or participation in track and field at Hunt Junior High. Bullat recalls Ted having more freedom than he did. "It seemed like he didn't have a lot of the restrictions," he said. Ted didn't seem to spend much time at home. He had some skiing buddies, or friends in Scouts or the church youth group, but they weren't invited to Ted's house. There was no hanging out in his room, which was in the basement of the North Skyline Drive home.

As a child, Ted had thrown tantrums because he was competing for his mother's now very divided attention. As a teenager, he had impulsive outbursts. Jerry Bullat still found Ted humorous and for the most part, good company on ski trips. Ted would pretend to have a British accent. Bullat thought he was trying to sound like "a New England elitist." "He always seemed a little more intense than the average guy," Bullat remembered. But he was a loner when it came to girls. By one account he was voted "shyest" in junior high school. He stuttered, although some childhood friends remember it as more, as a "horrible speech impediment." He was both a loner and a gregarious cut-up. He didn't date, but invited a popular girl to the prom. In fact, he seemed, even to his friends, a contradiction. He seemed to have more than one personality.

Ted was clever. On a ski trip during their junior year, he accidentally ran into a woman on a run. That spring, in Bullat's yearbook, Ted drew a line sketch of a downhill skier and wrote, "Stien strikes again. From one great skier to another. We've got one more year to wipe them old ladies of [*sic*] the ski slope." Ted signed his sketch Theodore Stien Ydnub. Ted was referring to the Norwegian Olympic skier,

Stein Ericksen, but misspelled Stein. Ydnub is—of course—Bundy spelled backwards.

He was an average student, but he was very good at some things, including stealing. After one trip to the mountains, he pulled into his parents' garage, forgetting the skis on the roof of his car (it wasn't the only time Ted would ruin skis driving in or out of a garage). They broke, and Ted was furious. But within days, he had completely new gear, the expensive stuff. Bullat was sure it was stolen. "He was a thief, he was resourceful," Bullat explained. Ted had no money, and Jerry was used to having to pay for everything when he and Ted were on a jaunt.

They would take Ted's car or the Wilson High School ski bus. Bullat would pay Ted's way. In return, Ted tutored Bullat in American Government. Bullat knew Ted was getting the better deal. "My parents always said I was gullible," he said. One of Ted's scams was making fake lift tickets for the ski slopes. Doug was terrible at shoplifting and always got caught, according to his sister Sandi, but Ted didn't get caught and would boast of sneaking into houses in the neighborhood and lifting money or items. Doug and Ted drifted apart during their high school years. Doug got into martial arts and body building; Ted's favorite pastimes were skiing and stealing.

From his earliest thefts—and there would be a lot of them over the years—Ted felt no remorse, no guilt, no nagging sense of responsibility, and no fear that he would be caught. Ted just didn't think like that. His brain didn't work that way. He did get caught a time or two. He was fired from a hotel for stealing from employee lockers. All his life Ted would steal cash because he always needed it (he seemed to be able to afford only a few dollars of gas at a time for his VW), but by college he had branched out and was shoplifting television sets, stereos, a Boston fern for his apartment (which he called "Fern" and took loving care of), another plant, a Ficus Benjamina (highly poisonous), tools and a tool chest, more ski clothes and ski boots, textbooks, cookware, art, a Navajo rug, dozens of pairs of socks at a time, credit cards, and really good cuts of steak.

Louise always said Ted's favorite book as a child was *Treasure Island.* But by the time he was a teenager, his tastes had changed to detective magazines, true crime, as well as pornography. Ted was fascinated with true crime stories and detective magazines, popular reading in America in the days before cable television and reenactments of crimes. (Author Ann Rule, who became a friend of his as his crime spree was beginning, wrote for some of the magazines in the 1970s.)

He might have read the July 1961 issue of *True Detective,* with a cover illustration depicting a visit to a Lover's Lane lookout gone bad. A man is busily tying a young woman's hands behind her back. Her boyfriend looks to be dead, slumped over the driver's side of his red T-bird convertible, and who knows what horrors await the girl.

Or maybe Ted read the next month's issue of *True Detective,* the very month Ann Marie Burr disappeared. Once again, a young woman—this time wearing just a swimsuit—looks frightened as she finds her boyfriend dead, sprawled on the back of what appears to be a wooden ski boat, maybe a Chris Craft. On this cover, the killer is out of sight but obviously lurking nearby, waiting to jump out and surprise the girl when she is at her most vulnerable.

The boyfriends may be dead, but they had money and good taste when alive.

While the titles of the magazine articles seemed as benign as a *Perry Mason* episode (*The Clue of the Discarded Nylons,* and *The Killer Liked Apple Pie* appear in those issues), Ted liked the magazines because some of them were graphic inside, with real crime scene photos of dead and sexually assaulted bodies (later, he called the magazines "very potent material"). Some of the titles of the articles could have described Ted's crimes, years later: *Bludgeoned Brunette in Butternut Creek,* and *Case of the Strangled Coed,* were featured in *True Detective* in 1966.

Ted could have followed the careers of Tacoma's two most-famous crime fighters, detectives Tony Zatkovich and Ted Strand, colorfully described in articles titled *Rendezvous With A Corpse* and *Let Me Lead You To His Grave* in magazines promising "authentic stories of crime detection." In April 1966, Ted could have read in *Master Detective* about a crime close to home. The headline to the story was: An Appeal to Master Detective Readers CAN YOU HELP FIND ANNE [*sic*] MARIE BURR?

Ted would be a police junkie the rest of his life (extremely common for serial killers). Beginning with the magazines and books on crime he could find at the library, he studied police procedures and how people got away with murder. It may have seemed to his parents that it was just another hobby—if they even knew of his interest in police work and murder. All Louise remembered was finding a copy of *Playboy* under his bed once or twice during his teenage years. (Many years later, after Ted's death, the FBI noted how he sometimes used his victims to re-enact scenarios on the covers of detective magazines.)

It wasn't until near the end of his life that Ted would describe the beginnings of what he called—with gross understatement—his "trouble" or his "problem." Referring to his teenage interest in peeping, Ted told journalist Stephen Michaud, "Again, this is something that a lot of young boys would do and without intending any harm, and that was basically where I was at the time. But I see how it later formed the basis for the so-called entity, that part of me that began to visualize and fantasize more violent things... " His fascination with sex and murder coincided with other changes in Ted. He didn't understand social interactions. "I didn't know what made things tick," he told Michaud. "I didn't know what made people want to be friends. I didn't know what made people attractive to one another. I didn't know what underlay social interactions." He had trouble completing things and so had a spotty and erratic college career and job history. He marveled at the ease with which his four half-siblings fit in. In high school he felt out of touch with his peers, including boys he had grown up with. He described himself as "stuck," and told Michaud, "In my early schooling, it seemed like there was no problem in learning what the appropriate social behaviors were. It just seemed like I hit a wall in high school." His explanation of those years is contradictory and secretive. In other words, pure Ted Bundy.

"It was not so much that there were significant events (in my boyhood), but the lack of things that took place was significant," Ted continued. "The omission of important developments. I felt that I had developed intellectually but not socially. In junior high, everything was fine. Even went to some parties. Nothing that I can recall happened that summer before my sophomore year to stunt me or otherwise hinder my progress. Emotionally and socially, something stunted my progress in high school. Not that I ever got into trouble. Or wanted to do anything wrong."

His friends complained that he would make plans with them, then not show up. Or he would come up behind them suddenly to scare them (he liked to strangle his victims from the rear, too). And Ted began prowling.

Ted would say of his teenage years, "I loved the darkness, the darkness would excite me, it was really sort of my ally, because I could creep around in the darkness." And, according to Sandi Holt, Ted was drinking heavily in high school; for the rest of his life alcohol would be a depressant that would prompt his spiraling moods and loosen his inhibitions so he could kill.

Eventually, Ted began thinking and speaking of his behavior in a detached way. He hinted that he began murdering young. Maybe that's what he meant when he said that "something happened" when he was a teenager. He could mention his crimes, but only in the third person. "The first victim of this other person could have been an 8 or 9-year-old girl," he told an expert on serial killers. It was a round-about way of confessing without confessing, one more way to titillate and manipulate the police, yet remain in charge.

The Bundy's must have read or heard about the little girl missing in their former neighborhood. The news coverage of the search for Ann Burr was on the front page of the Tacoma newspaper every day, and was covered by the two Seattle newspapers, as well as local radio and television. Sandi Holt heard the news on the radio and burst into tears, telling her mother that she knew the little girl who had vanished.

Even if Louise was house-bound by her fifth pregnancy, she had to have known that just two blocks from where she and Teddy had lived with her uncle, a child had likely been abducted. She had children about the same age. Bev had put up missing posters at grocery stores all over town. The compelling posters, with big lettering and the haunting photo of Ann, were everywhere. Ted was a paperboy for one of the Seattle papers. Did Louise empathize with the mother of the missing girl? Ted's friend, Jerry Bullat, remembers his own mother being distraught about Ann's disappearance. So were the parents of the other children who played with Ann and parents with children attending Grant Elementary. Sandi Holt's mother immediately kept a closer rein on Sandy, and Doug was ordered to walk her to Geiger Elementary when the new school year began.

Over the years, Bev Burr and Louise Bundy would meet by accident. They didn't speak, but they had a lot in common. They were petite, they kept their hair style simple and wore no makeup, and they were intelligent. They were married to working-class men, and both had five children. Each would lose her oldest child, the one with the most promise, in a horrific way. And at the most stressful times in their lives, they coped in the same way: they offered guests apple pie.

In 1961, Ted was getting ready to begin ninth grade at Hunt Junior High. As Tacoma police questioned hundreds of teenagers and men (two of their prime suspects being just 13 and 15 years old) about the disappearance of Ann Burr, there were thousands more they didn't know. The name Ted Bundy didn't come to their attention because he didn't live in the north end of the city, and Ted's family was Methodist; the Burrs and most of their friends and neighbors—all potential suspects—attended St. Patrick's. Although he roamed and peeped, Ted wouldn't be known to Tacoma police until a few years later, when he reportedly was picked up on suspicion of auto theft and burglary.

Those records were reportedly expunged while he was still a juvenile.

In the summer of 1961, Ted was 14 years old; he would turn 15 in November. He told Dr. Dorothy Otnow Lewis that when he was ... "twelve, fourteen, fifteen... in the summer... something happened, something, I'm not sure what it was... I would fantasize about coming up to some girl sunbathing in the woods, or something innocuous like that... I was beginning to get involved in what they would call, developed a preference for what they call, autoerotic sexual activity," he told her. "A portion of my personality was not fully... it began to emerge... by the time I realized how powerful it was, I was in big trouble... "

Ted's favorite subject was Ted. He loved to talk. A state Republican party leader who got to know Ted said he had "the gift of gab" and "oozed sincerity." One advantage to being on death row for years is that many sought him out, and he could expound on his theories, including that of killers who begin young. "Perhaps the only firm trend I ever ran across in the study of abnormal behavior," Ted told a journalist, "was that the younger that a person... that he or she was when they manifested abnormal behavior or thought pattern... the more likely it was that there was going to be a condition that would be lasting. And, uh, permanent. A chronic disorder."

Later, when the police, the media, and the Burrs wondered if Ted could have begun his killing with one small girl, a girl who didn't fit the image of the college coeds he killed (although the last girl he killed was just 12, and there were a couple of 14 year olds, too), a young girl who wasn't in college and didn't have long hair parted in the middle, Louise Bundy went on the defensive. She told the Tacoma News Tribune, "I resent the fact that everybody in Tacoma thinks just because he lived in Tacoma he did that one too, way back when he was 14. I'm sure he didn't. We were such a close family... he didn't have anything against little girls."

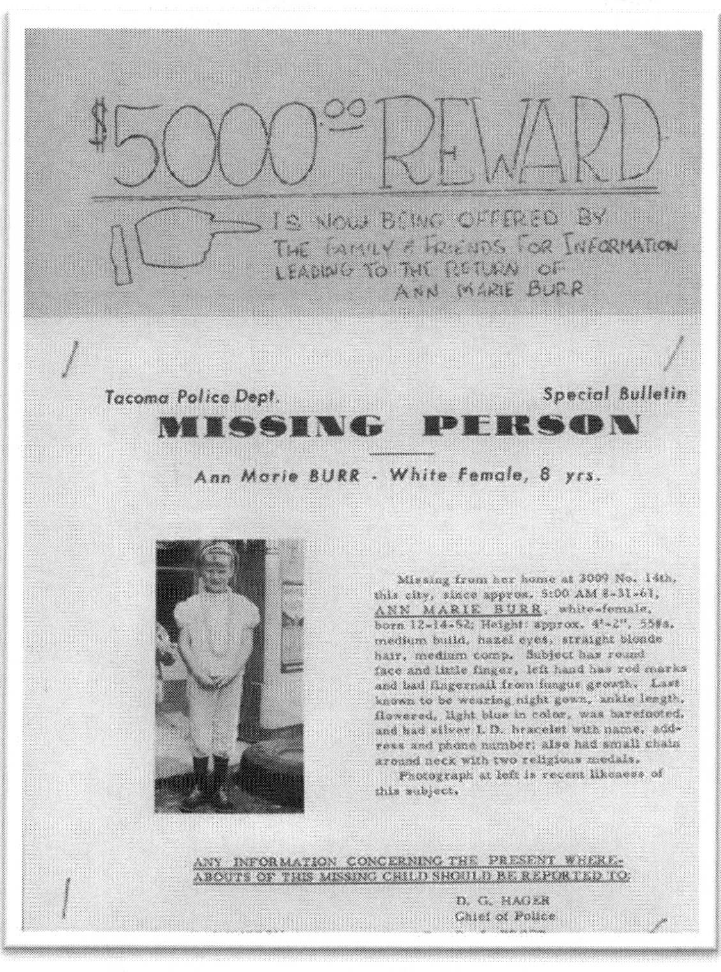

$5000.00 REWARD

IS NOW BEING OFFERED BY THE FAMILY & FRIENDS FOR INFORMATION LEADING TO THE RETURN OF ANN MARIE BURR

Tacoma Police Dept. Special Bulletin

MISSING PERSON

Ann Marie BURR - White Female, 8 yrs.

Missing from her home at 3009 No. 14th, this city, since approx. 5:00 AM 8-31-61, ANN MARIE BURR, white-female, born 12-14-52; Height: approx. 4'-2", 55#s, medium build, hazel eyes, straight blonde hair, medium comp. Subject has round face and little finger, left hand has red marks and bad fingernail from fungus growth. Last known to be wearing night gown, ankle length, flowered, light blue in color, was barefooted, and had silver I. D. bracelet with name, address and phone number; also had small chain around neck with two religious medals.

Photograph at left is recent likeness of this subject.

ANY INFORMATION CONCERNING THE PRESENT WHEREABOUTS OF THIS MISSING CHILD SHOULD BE REPORTED TO:

D. G. HAGER
Chief of Police

The missing poster created August 31, 1961.

Beverly Burr's father, Roy Leach,on the porch of his Tacoma grocery store.

Bev's sixth grade class at Central Elementary School in 1939. Bev is third from left in the front row. Her friend Haruye Kawano is second from right in the front row.

Bev, at left, as yearbook editor,
Stadium High School, 1945-46.

'll Wed in July

The article announcing Bev's engagement to Don Burr, 1951.

Bev, pregnant with Ann, on an Oregon beach in 1952.

The four Burr children at Christmas, probably 1959.

Beverly Burr, with Mary, Julie, Greg, and Ann on Fox Island. Summer, 1960, one year before Ann disappeared.

The four Burr children, in outfits Bev had sewn, possibly Easter, 1961.

Newspaper photo of search party. Don Burr is second from the left. Sept. 2, 1961.

Police photographs of the Burr house and Ann's bedroom.

Bev's mother, Marie Leach, offers a reward.

hey'll Hunt A Lifetime For Ann Marie

145 Days Of Heartbreak

Detective Team Talks With Missing Girl's Parents

Ted Strand, Bev Burr, Don Burr, and Tony Zatkovich mark 145 days of searching for Ann. January 23, 1962.

The cover of Master Detective, April, 1966.

An appeal
to MASTER DETECTIVE readers:

CAN YOU HELP FIND
ANN MARIE BURR?

Tacoma, Washington police, and the family of a pretty little girl who vanished in the night, urgently request the aid of any alert reader who thinks he or she might have information that could possibly unravel the mystery of this tragic and baffling disappearance . . .

The article in Master Detective, April, 1966, written by Robert Cour, of the Seattle Post-Intelligencer.

Newspaper coverage of the adoption. Bev, Greg, and Mary feeding the new baby, Laura, July 18, 1963.

Bev's mother, Marie, with George Voigt on their wedding day. They are holding Laura.

Bev and Don on Fox Island, with Barney, Ann's cocker spaniel, 1962.

Greg, Mary, and Julie, one year after Ann disappeared, 1962.

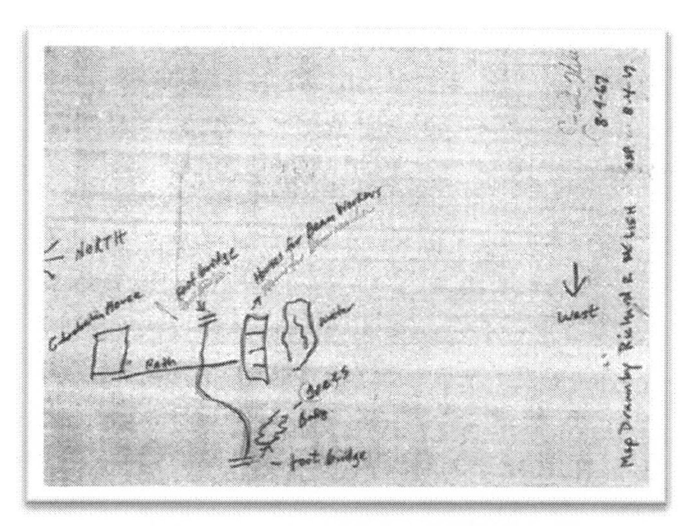

The 1967 sketch of the Oregon field where Richard Raymond McLish says he buried Ann's body.

The house on North 28th Street, in the mid-1970s.

5

The Weekend

THE YOUNG POLICE OFFICER, APPARENTLY CHOSEN because he was agile, had one leg in and one leg out of Beverly Burr's living room window. She couldn't bear to watch. If he could maneuver into the house without breaking her collection of English pottery Toby jugs, without getting tangled in the TV antenna or leaving a fingerprint or a clue, then it made the possibility that an intruder had taken her daughter both more plausible and more baffling.

Instead of watching the officer, Bev kept her eye on the pottery displayed on the table immediately under the window, each one a caricature of a short, fat fellow seated with a jug on his knee. Their cheery grins taunted Bev.

The police were back to take another look inside the Burr house. They were still monitoring phone calls in the basement, there was still a patrol car each night on the street in front of the house, and they were busy chasing down tips and known sex offenders. But were they *certain* there was no evidence of an intruder? Just to be sure, the forensics team returned, hoping to add to their pitifully small cache, which consisted of the lone red thread and the toe print on the outdoor bench.

They took more photos of the outside of the house, and tried to get fingerprints off a downspout that Don had told them about. It had been pulled loose from a gutter on the northwest corner and might have been used as a handhold. It was beneath Greg's bedroom window (who was asleep in the basement that night). There were no fingerprints on the southwest window, which they thought was the way the kidnapper had entered the house. Then they searched the living room again; it was the living room, and the window, the Toby jugs, the doors, and the furniture that should hold clues.

Late that night, the young, agile officer and his partner wrote in their report that the latest search was in vain. It was too late to find clues that might have been overlooked. There would be no latent fingerprint. A well-meaning relative of the Burrs had dusted the living room, top to bottom.

Bob Drost was the only member of the police force who believed Ann was alive. He thought she had been taken by someone she knew (that's why the family didn't hear any screams), someone who was desperate to have a little girl, someone who didn't live in Tacoma and could raise Ann without the family knowing or others becoming suspicious. Someone who—he went so far as to say—"cherished" the little girl, yet was busy brainwashing Ann. He didn't think it would take long for an eight-year-old to forget her family and cleave to a new one. Whoever abducted Ann, Drost said, didn't leave "five cents worth of clues." He described the result of the investigation as "a handful of nothing—it was like grabbing clouds."

Drost was Captain of Detectives and had been away with his family on their annual fishing and camping trip to Lake Chelan, three hours east in the central part of the state. He returned to the biggest missing persons case since the Weyerhaeuser and Mattson kidnappings. But this case was more puzzling. The Weyerhaeuser boy was kidnapped off a city street, and a ransom demand came quickly. And Charles Mattson's siblings saw him taken from their house; his body was found two weeks later. But with the Ann Marie Burr case there was no evidence, no witnesses, no body, and no credible ransom demand.

The newspapers reported that police could find no proof that anyone had entered the house. They were told there was no sign of a struggle in Ann's bedroom. Ann's disappearance was still not officially considered an abduction.

Drost was friends with Detectives Zatkovich and Strand, but especially Tony Zatkovich. Tony's brother Al had married a close friend of Drost's wife, Betty, and they considered themselves family—the kind of extended family that got together for Thanksgiving and birthdays. Drost had been a member of the same vigilante group of police as Detectives Strand and Zatkovich. When he got back from fishing, Drost officially put into place the major roles in the investigation: Strand and Zatkovich would be the lead detectives; Det. Richard Roberts would be in charge of the underground search, including the city sewer system; Police Inspector Emil Smith was overall search director.

Part of the detective's job was to get to know as much about Ann as they could. They found that opinions of Ann varied greatly. Her grandmother, Marie Leach, had told police she thought Ann was "a little irrational." Ann spent time with Becky B__ who lived a block away. Both of Becky's parents worked, so the children would often spend time with Mrs. B__ 's mother during the day. Becky had seen Ann on Wednesday. "I last saw Ann in the neighborhood between 5 p.m. and 6 p.m. the evening before she disappeared. I think Ann has quite a temper and she throws tantrums," Becky told police. Becky's mother, a schoolteacher, said she considered herself "very good friends" with the Burr family. "It is my impression that she (Ann) is the favorite in the family. She most always gets what she wants and is very high in intelligence for a girl of her age. I feel the family is a little lax in the child's activities, as to staying with other friends overnight or staying for dinner at their home," Mrs. B__ told the police.

Her uncle Raleigh considered Ann "brilliant." Ann gave off a confidence that could be misconstrued in a child. It could be mistaken as flirtatiousness. Her cousin, Eddie Cavallo, was 14 years old when she disappeared. "She was a little sweetheart," he says. "She was like a teddy bear; you wanted to give her a little squeeze. She attracted males; she elicited a response from boys. She was a very sexual little kid. It was the way she was wired."

Both the family and police knew the clock was ticking. "Hopes for the safe return of the missing youngster, believed to be barefoot and clad in only an ankle-length nightgown, continued to wane," the Tacoma News Tribune reported. Over the Labor Day weekend, more than 600 men from the Army's 2nd Battle Group, 39th Infantry, stationed at Ft. Lewis, and National Guardsmen from Camp Murray staged a massive ground search. It was too windy to take a helicopter up, but they covered 700-acre Point Defiance Park on foot, a mostly undeveloped wilderness in the middle of urban sprawl. Point Defiance was where the last, or one of the last, photographs of Ann was taken. Bev had taken Ann to the park's zoo so she could feed the goats.

A number of Tacoma residents had dusted off their Ouija boards—a popular Christmas item the year before, by now relegated to the hall closet. They called police to say Ann was safe; Ann was far away from Tacoma by now; Ann was somewhere at Point Defiance Park. When the winds did let up, an Army pilot and a Tacoma police officer used a helicopter to cover the park from the air. They flew over its beaches, cliffs, wooded areas, boat house, and sewer outfall. They went as low as they could over Commencement Bay and "The Narrows," what folks called the Tacoma Narrows Bridge, which connects the city and the Kitsap Peninsula.

A dream took Alfred S__ from his home in Seattle to Tacoma, via a Greyhound bus. From the bus station he took a taxi to the Burr house. The 79-year-old man told Bev and Don that he had had a vision or a religious revelation that Ann was being kept in the back bedroom of a white house with green trim. He stated that the Lord had provided the vision, and the Lord had even provided an address, 4548 Pearl Street. Detectives Johnson and Six took Mr. S__ to the police station where he told his story again. Then they put him on a bus back to Seattle. Bev asked the police to check out 4548 Pearl Street. There was no house at 4548 Pearl Street; there was a Piggly Wiggly grocery store under construction. There were several white houses with green trim nearby, but they decided it wasn't worth knocking on the doors.

Over the holiday weekend, the police returned to homes in North Tacoma that hadn't been searched earlier. Detectives, in old clothes and with flashlights, meticulously crawled under houses and into attics.

The town's Public Works Department began combing the main sewer lines near the Burr house. A three man crew went underground "using portable lights to probe the pitch black flumes of the city's sewer network through the North End," the Tacoma News Tribune told its readers who were following the search for Ann. At low tide, volunteer scuba divers went to the end of the line—the main outfall pipe on Commencement Bay, not far from Tacoma's favorite night spot, The Top of the Ocean—where the rushing flow of storm drainage and sewage was rapid enough to push a body out the pipe and into the bay. But it hadn't. Man holes and catch basins were searched and two muddy ponds in

Buckley Gulch, which ran just a block from the Burr house, were drained. Citizen volunteers searched the nearby city of Fircrest, focusing on the construction site of a stadium for the town's minor league baseball team, the Tacoma Giants.

When no trace of the girl was found, Det. Richard Roberts was asked what came next. "I just don't know where we go from here," he said. Tacoma Police Inspector Smith called it one of the most baffling cases in Tacoma crime files.

On September 3, the fourth day after Ann vanished, the city did what Don suggested just hours after Ann went missing; it sent men to search the ditches being dug at the University of Puget Sound. Don had worried that it was a feasible place to leave a child's body. The digging in question was in an area on the western edge of the campus, running along Union Avenue for several blocks between Adams Street and Washington Street. The five fraternities (to be known as the Union Avenue Housing), would be connected by an underground tunnel and would share a common kitchen, also underground.

There's no record of whether the police shared the bad news with Bev and Don. By the time they went to search the excavation sites, they couldn't find any ditches with water. "At this time, all ditches are covered and the roads are open," the police report noted. Traffic was driving over the spot where Don thought the body of his daughter might have been cruelly discarded.

By Sunday, police had administered polygraphs to nearly 30 men and boys. One was 13-year-old Terry M__, who lived about a block from the Burrs. A year before, Terry had been arrested for window peeping at the college and taken to Remann Hall, the juvenile detention center and school. What the police found especially intriguing as they took another look at him was that he liked to peep early, before 6 a.m. His family attended St. Patrick's, he knew Ann, and his younger brother played with her. Terry had been to the Burrs' many times, but claimed to never have been inside the home.

Terry's father was furious with the police. Just because his son had been picked up for peeping when he was 12, the police were trying to hang Ann Burr's disappearance on him. Besides, the father said, window peeping is normal; a lot of boys do it.

But the police were intrigued with all the questions the boy asked about the case. Terry asked them as many questions as they asked of him. Did they have any evidence? He mused over his own theories with the police: it must have been a prowler. Were the searchers wearing gloves? Not to preserve evidence, but in case they had to comb through raspberry and blueberry bushes which were so fierce in the Northwest they could rip your skin off? The police concluded Terry was just as good a suspect as anyone else.

Detectives were going to the shoe stores in town, trying to track down a boy's or men's tennis shoe that matched the print on the Burr's bench. They might have been Keds, but they had an unusual tread; that was their best clue so far. They withheld the information from the newspapers; a teenager, or even his parents, might hastily dispose of tennis shoes with an unusual sole.

The police finally got 15-year-old Robert Bruzas down to the police station. "It had been brought to our attention previously that Robert associated more with the younger children than those around his own age group," Detectives Strand and Zatkovich wrote. Robert had been a *Tribune* paper boy for the last 13 months, a substitute carrier before that, and he was also working at the college swimming pool two blocks west. They asked him about his friends (one was Terry M__) their ages, and if he had ever kissed the 17-year-old girl that he admitted liking. He said no. Robert admitted playing with Ann and the other young girls in the neighborhood, "probably because none of the boys around his age were in that immediate vicinity. Another reason was that he liked the children." He told the detectives that on the afternoon before Ann disappeared, he saw her and her friend Susie as he was on his way to pick up his newspapers. Then, police gave him a polygraph. He did *not* pass.

Two days later, on the first day of his sophomore year at Stadium High School (where Bev Burr had edited the yearbook and set her sights on being a professional writer), the detectives pulled Robert out of an afternoon class, and took him to the police department for a second round of tough questioning. Detectives Strand and Zatkovich—who liked to "kick a juvenile in the ass and send him home"—did a job on Robert. With no parents or lawyers present, "They told me I was lying," Robert Bruzas said years later. "I was pretty naïve, and I was scared." They hammered him with questions and reminded him he had failed a polygraph two days before. Then they drove him home, and told his mother, Alice, that they wanted Robert to speak with Father Godley at St. Patrick's, where the Bruzas and Burr families worshipped. His mother agreed he would. Neighbors offered the family the name of an attorney.

The next day, the detectives paid a visit to the priest. Father Godley hadn't met with Robert yet, but another priest had. Father Godley told them he didn't know if he would still meet with Robert. After all, he reminded them, what would be the point? Anything the teenager would tell him, any *confession*, would be kept in confidence.

The detectives were finding Father Godley elusive. Whether because of the confidentiality of the priest-congregant relationship, or wanting to distance the parish from the tragedy, he was not being particularly helpful to the police. The police had wanted to search the church the day Ann went missing, and they did. But when they inquired about a child molester thought to hang around the church, they didn't get much help. They staked out the church, sending a plainclothes cop to mass, but he didn't spot the man they were looking for. When the priest called on the grieving family, Bev did what she often did: she documented the occasion with a photograph, and served him apple pie.

In the photo, the priest is sitting comfortably in an oversized chair, smiling broadly; on either side of him are Julie and Mary, also smiling. Hanging on the wall in back of them is a print of the iconic painting of Jesus, "The Head of Christ," by Warner Sallman. An angry showdown between Father Godley and Don was yet to come.

In their report, Strand and Zatkovich wrote that although Robert passed a second polygraph and "denied having any immoral ideas in reference to the children," they still considered him "a likely suspect."

Robert's father and older brother were also questioned and took polygraphs. The police were especially thorough searching the Bruzas house. Still, sometime over the weekend, when the Bruzas family was scattered and no one was home, Bev Burr went to the back door. Unlike the Burrs, who always locked up, the Bruzas' didn't lock their doors, so Bev went right on in.

She had to see for herself. She searched the main floor and the upstairs, where the children slept. She didn't risk taking the time to search the basement or the attic. There was no sign of Ann, no St. Christopher bracelet that might have been worn by a small girl, no red sweater with a snag in one of the children's rooms.

Both Don and Bev would be asked to confront their pasts in the days after Ann vanished. For Don, his relationship with his father over the sale of the logging company and with his mother over his taking Catholic instruction were barely healed wounds. For Bev, it was facing what life might have been if she hadn't married Don. She gave the police the name of a man who had loved her and offered to give up everything for her: Larry M__ .

Bev was well-read and knew what was going on in the world. Two years earlier she had read about the Clutters, the Kansas family murdered by two petty thieves who thought the wealthy farmer kept money in his house (the case was immortalized by Truman Capote in his book, *In Cold Blood*). Bev thought of the Clutters when Ann was taken.

"We could have all been shot. Who were they after?" she asked, referring to the person or persons who broke into her home. "Were they after a certain one of us or not? Who were they after?" She had also read of Candy Rogers, the nine-year-old Spokane girl who had disappeared March 6, 1959, while selling Camp Fire Girl mints. Ann was a Camp Fire Girl too and sold mints. During the search for Candy Rogers, three Air Force servicemen died when their helicopter struck an electric line and plunged into the Spokane River. Sixteen days after the girl disappeared, she was found raped and murdered. Her murder was never solved. Her father could not live with the tragedy, and killed himself four years later.

Bev and Don Burr, as well as the police, were frustrated by the few ransom calls they received.

Bev: *Hello. Hello?*

Call: *Hello. Who is this speaking, please?*

Bev: *This is Mrs. Burr speaking.*

Call: *Ah.*

Bev: *Hello*

Call: *Hello*

Bev: *Yes.*

Call: *Is your daughter missin'?*

Bev: *Yes, she is gone.*

Call: *If you'd like to have your daughter back I want $5,000 in cash by tomorrow night.*

Bev: *Well, I don't... can you tell us how and what to do, please? Can you tell us what to do, please?*

Call: *Drive by the park in Tacoma.*

Bev: *What park is it? Which park do you mean? Hello?*

Call: *Hello.*

Bev: *Did you say to do what?*

Call: *The park off of J Street.*

Bev: *The park off of J Street. There isn't any park... you mean Wright's Park or which park?*

Call: *Wright's Park.*

Bev: *Wright's Park, that one near downtown?*

Call: *Right, drive south by 3 o'clock tomorrow afternoon. Five thousand dollars in cash, that's all.*

Bev: *Well, I don't understand what you mean.*

Call: *That's all.*

Bev: *Well, where do you mean? Hello? Hello? Hello?*

Wright Park—its real name—is in North Tacoma, just a few blocks from the apartment where Ann's maternal grandmother, Marie Leach, lived. Since the late 1800s, the citizens of Tacoma could take the streetcar to the "English Style" park. In its glory days, there was lawn bowling, Fourth of July celebrations, Easter egg hunts, and "peaceful ponds" where swans glided in the summer, and college students skated in winter. By the late 1950s and early 1960s, the park went the way of other urban parks, and picked up a new name—Wright Park became known as "Fright Park."

Detectives Zatkovich and Strand went to Bev and Don's house the morning after the ransom call. The detectives must have had their doubts about its validity, because they asked Bev and Don if they wanted the police to stake out the park, and by the way, would they want to go along? Bev and Don declined. A plainclothes officer spent hours at the park but never found the caller.

The police did involve Don in the next ransom demand. Don had received a call from a man who said he was an ex-con so couldn't give his name, and that he had been in a prisoner-of-war camp during World War II. He claimed he had information about Ann—she was alive, but not in the state. He needed "one or two hundred dollars for expenses" to go retrieve her. The man asked Don to meet him at the Greyhound bus depot and to wear a light colored top coat and carry a hat under his right arm. Don got out his light gray coat and put his brown hat under his arm and met the man at the bus depot. So did

Detectives Strand and Zatkovich. They arrested Neal L__, whose only address was the Veterans Hospital on Seattle's Beacon Hill. He denied contacting Don, but they found the Burr's phone number on two items in his pocket.

Five days after Ann disappeared, Bev fastened the Superman cape onto Greg's shoulders. She was relieved that he could still be excited about his first day of kindergarten. This is what she wanted, she reminded herself, to help her children still experience the childhood they deserved. She and Mary walked Greg and Julie (now in second grade) to Grant School in the morning, and in the afternoon they were outside, ready to see them home. She would not let them walk alone, as she had let Ann.

That morning, Bev noticed activity she tried to distract the children from seeing. The Labor Day weekend had delayed garbage pickup, and now the trucks were rumbling through the neighborhood. Police had only done a cursory look at containers within a radius of several blocks of the Burr residence. Now the crews on the garbage trucks citywide had been asked to look closely for a small body or a blue and white flowered nightgown. They found a child's nightgown, and police took it to show Bev, but it wasn't Ann's.

Bev missed Ann terribly; she should have been walking with them, the eldest, the leader, the star pupil, the pianist, the artist. Bev had reread many times the comments from Ann's teacher at the end of the previous school year. The girl's second-grade teacher, Esther Reilly, called Ann an excellent student, a good reader, capable and dependable, creative, well-liked by all the children, and a joy to have in the room. The report ended with the teacher predicting Ann would have a very happy year in third grade.

6
145 Days

In recognition of the most widespread manhunt in Tacoma history, the disappearance of Ann Marie Burr was selected by the editors and reporters of the Tacoma News Tribune as the top news story of 1961—bigger than the resignation of Police Chief Roy Kerr (after a disagreement with the new city manager); bigger than the crash of a military jet immediately after takeoff from nearby McChord Air Force Base, killing 18 servicemen on board; bigger that the Tacoma Giants winning the Pacific Coast League pennant.

But first came the fall, and Ann's birthday, and then Christmas.

Bev's mother, Marie—who had finally realized that her granddaughter Ann wasn't being willful and hiding, but was gone—put up one thousand dollars for a reward. Bev and Don added to it as did some community groups and the amount climbed to five thousand dollars. A photograph in the newspaper publicizing the reward showed Marie, Bev, and Ann's dog, Barney. The story said the family hoped the reward would "spur some new development in the mysterious Aug. 31 disappearance of the pretty, blonde girl," and reiterated that, despite the bench that had been moved and the window and door found open, police still had no proof that anyone had entered the house. The story tried to put to rest gossip that Bev and Don were away for part of the evening and were to blame for their daughter's disappearance. But the rumors persisted. Some of Bev's friends went around town, asking for contributions to the reward money. One time, Bev was with a friend who approached the owner of a small hardware store. "Hell, I wouldn't donate a dime!" he declared. "There's no mystery about that girl. The Burrs themselves know where she is." Bev left the store without identifying herself.

Soon, new versions of the missing posters—with the photograph of Ann, somber, wearing her lei—had an awkwardly drawn addition: a hand, with one finger pointing to lettering announcing:

$5000 REWARD Is Now Being Offered By The Family & Friends for Information Leading To The Return Of Ann Marie Burr.

Late at night after the children were asleep, Bev and Don worked at the dining room table, taping the hand with the pointing finger onto the posters (now reminiscent of Uncle Sam ordering young men to enlist in the Army).

There was rarely a day without an update in the newspapers. In October, Bev and Don asked residents of Tacoma to search their property again and urged hunters to be on the lookout as deer season approached.

On the day before Thanksgiving, Bev wrote an "open letter, in the spirit of Thanksgiving Day," to her daughter's kidnapper. It was printed in the Seattle Post-*Intelligencer* along with an update on the case. In a photograph accompanying the story, three-year-old Mary—too young to remember if she saw her sister taken three months before—is sucking the knuckles on her right hand as she sits on Bev's lap. There's a Bible open, as if Bev had been reading to Mary. In the letter Bev wrote:

> *"If the one who took our little girl is reading this, will you think about what Jesus said about those who sinned against Him: 'There will be joy in heaven over one sinner who repents, more than over ninety-nine just persons who have no need of repentance.' Luke 15, 1-10. We pray that you will have the strength to come forward and confess; tell us, her mother and father, where she is."*

Detective Ted Strand, a Camel dangling from one hand, had the other on the wheel of the 1958, white Chevy with Oregon plates. It was Dec. 8 and he was driving Mrs. Leone M. Teeters around Tacoma. He kept a tape recorder going to capture her thoughts about where Ann Burr might be.

"I have a peculiar, nervous feeling, and I feel like I want to cry," the psychic told Strand. The department had been contacted by dozens of psychics, and to be kind to Bev, the detectives listened to most of them. Bev would rule out no possible source of information. Bev herself had given a man a small cup Ann often drank out of, for him to use when he went searching with his divining rod.

She turned down another man's request for a pair of Ann's socks, but only because she assumed he was going to use a tracking dog and a dog would need a scent. All of Ann's clothes were clean when she disappeared so there were no socks, nothing with a lingering scent of the girl.

Mrs. Teeters, from Seattle, had had visions of a dark green Chevrolet being parked near the Burr's the night Ann vanished. She had also "seen" in her vision a two-story white house next to a brown house. Because the population of Tacoma was nearly 148,000 and the town was composed of mostly single-family residences, looking for a two-story white house next to a brown house seemed like the hunt for the proverbial needle in a haystack. But Strand drove Mrs. Teeters for hours, first north from the Burr's, then eventually turning south at her direction, making a loop that took them by the Allenmoore Public Golf Course, where she said she felt "bothered." Strand told her that a body of a 32-year-old man had been found there a few weeks before. Then she changed her mind, and they looked for a house standing alone with empty lots on both sides. Near the end of their outing Mrs. Teeters said she believed Ann was alive, would be found within three months, but was not in Tacoma. The police, she said, would have to go "far afield" to find the girl.

The newspaper updates did elicit new tips. Mrs. Evelyn K___, of Oak Harbor, Washington, telephoned Tacoma police to say that on a trip from Alaska, through Canada, across Montana, and into

Idaho in early September, she had spoken with a young girl with a hurt finger. Mrs. K__ and her husband had pulled over at a one-pump service station for a snack; it might have been a Texaco station, but it could have been a Standard Oil station. The girl was with a man and a woman and another child. "She came around the end of the counter to talk to us. She wanted to go with us in our camper... there was something wrong with a fingernail on the left hand." Mrs. K__ went on to say that the couple didn't like the girl talking to them, and were "...unnecessarily rough with her... (the woman) grasped for her and sort of shook her around... "

The police had her repeat details about the girl's hurt finger. It seemed to be the same finger that Bev Burr treated with mercurochrome on the night Ann disappeared. But the police were skeptical of finding the gas station. Mrs. K__ wasn't sure if she was in Montana or Idaho at the time.

In the Pacific Northwest and across western Canada there were reports of small girls crying that they wanted to go home to their mommy and daddy. In British Columbia; at Harts Lake at the foot of Mt. Rainier; at a roadside motel hundreds of miles to the east on the other side of Washington state; and soon at the Seattle World's Fair, young blonde girls would plead with strangers to take them home.

Don had offered to take a second polygraph test. Detectives Strand and Zatkovich didn't think Don was hiding anything, but they continued to question him intensely. Don told police he thought his neighbor Mr. E__, Susie's father, should take a test, too. In trying to reconstruct the evening Ann had vanished, Don remembered hearing what he thought was the E's__ garage at a late hour. And Don had another suggestion: that Father Godley, the priest at St. Patrick's, take a polygraph.

Detective Strand and Lt. Richardson paid the priest a visit. They talked with him about his impressions of the Burr family and then asked, would the priest "subject himself" to a polygraph? It wasn't a surprise to the priest. He had known for weeks that Don wanted him to take the test, and Father Godley admitted to the police that he had been "boiling mad" ever since. The priest told them that "a man in his position is not likely to be questioned as a suspect as he is a man of God and is trying to save lives rather than destroy them." He told them that he had worked hard to "bring the Burr family together in the Catholic life" by baptizing the children. And he had tolerated—and tried to help—the family during the dust-up over Don's taking Catholic instruction. Then, in a huff, the priest explained to the police that he had done so much for them, and yet he hadn't seen them in church since the baptisms. He had endured the questions about Robert Bruzas and the police stakeout of the church in hopes of finding a predator thought to be hanging around. But asking him to take a polygraph was too much. He said it was against the laws of the church, and furthermore the Bishop would never allow it. And then he added this concern: if word ever got out to the congregation that a priest had submitted to a lie detector test, his reputation would be ruined on account of the gossip.

He concluded his interview with the police by saying that "in his own mind he knew that he was innocent and any thought to the contrary was ridiculous." Police ran a credit check on Don and Bev. "The Burr's have an excellent credit rating," they wrote in their report, adding that as a logger in California, Don was "classified as a satisfactory person... in State of Oregon, was highly regarded." They talked to the Burr's dentist and doctors; all said that the parents were affectionate with their children.

Every December 14, Bev threw a birthday party for Ann. Before she was school age, the guests were her young cousins and neighborhood friends. Bev chronicled each party in Ann's green album with "Baby's First Seven Years" embossed on the front. As if she had had a premonition that there would be no others, Bev had made the most of the album, squeezing eight years out of it. The prior year, for what would be Ann's last birthday party on December 14, 1960, 12 girls came home with Ann after school. They played games, including Bingo. Bev and Don gave their daughter "Tammy," her big doll, and clothes for her, including the matching nightgown Bev had sewn. Ann also received a book about Bluebirds, which she had just joined, a jewelry case, and several coloring sets. Each girl attending the party received a Christmas "prize." Bev made a dessert she called "Apple Santa," baked with the fruit from Mrs. Gustafson's small orchard next door.

A year later, on December, 14, 1961, on what would have been Ann's ninth birthday, there was no party. There were no children celebrating. There were no games. Bev wept in private.

She grieved the death of Ann's canary, the aging of her dog Barney, the change of seasons, and the day-by-day adjustments of life without Ann.

Bev tried to rally as Christmas approached. She had to give her other children some kind of Christmas. She shopped for gifts, sewed, baked, and held her breath that Ann might be home for Christmas. On Christmas Eve morning, the telephone rang. The tape recorder in the basement recorded the call. The caller said a man who worked at the Annie Wright Seminary in Tacoma (a boarding school founded to give the daughters of pioneers a Christian education) had taken Ann, or knew where she was. The caller was arrested three days later; he was a disgruntled janitor trying to get even with the boss who had recently fired him.

The credible ransom demands, the clues, the evidence, the leads that the police and the family thought were sure to develop and lead them to Ann, never materialized. There were a few foolish men, cranks trying to cash in on the search for the girl. They all asked for a few hundred dollars, not the full reward. Police never solved the mystery of the man dressed as a woman who Julie said talked to her and asked where she lived, just hours before Ann disappeared. They never found the midget with a beard one neighbor had reported seeing. They did find Carl B__ who was trying to interest homeowners in building a bomb shelter. He had boasted to others at the construction company where he worked that he had seen the missing girl. He told police that he had been in the Burr's neighborhood and saw a girl dressed only in a flimsy, pink dress, carrying a doll as she walked north in the wind and rain.

Police concluded he was "a strange person... somewhat of a loner... more of a hanger on than an employee" of the construction company. He told police his wife had shot at him once as he entered his home via a window. He, in turn, had applied for a concealed weapons permit and had been turned down. They gave Mr. B__ a polygraph exam. The results were negative.

Police thought their one real lead might be the print of the tennis shoe. Detectives took the mold of the shoe print they found in the yard to Soines Shoe Store, at North 26th and Proctor, apparently the only store in Tacoma that sold the "gym type shoe" with the unusual tread. Soines said the shoe was about the size of a teenager's foot, or a small man. The police were given the names of five families, and questioned a nine-year-old boy who owned a pair of the shoes. An 18-year-old had also purchased the shoes, but the police never questioned him because he had left for college in California. There is no record what they learned from the others who had purchased the shoes.

Donald F. Burr, the architect, continued to believe that his daughter Debra Sue had been the intended target. If it wasn't a scheme of her birthmother's, then maybe it was by someone who knew that the architect designed many homes and schools and was making a good living.

On January 23, 1962, the Seattle Post-*Intelligencer's* headline read: "145 Days of Heartbreak: They'll Hunt a 'Lifetime' for Ann Marie." Pictured are Bev and Don, seated in their living room with Ted Strand beside Bev and Tony Zatkovich leaning over Don and pointing to a calendar in Bev's lap. As if any of them needed to be reminded how much time had passed.

One hundred and forty-five days of swimming through sewers, crawling under houses, mailing twenty thousand posters with Ann's photograph to law enforcement agencies. One hundred and forty-five sleepless nights for Bev and Don, nights spent talking with Julie after the other children had gone to bed. Julie, at seven, was the most distressed of the children and felt the loss of her older sister—her best friend—keenly. She was in second grade at Grant elementary School, where Ann should have been right down the hall in a third-grade classroom.

Julie was aware that everyone was talking about Ann's disappearance; Julie felt pitied, and she did not want to be pitied. A classmate of Julie's remembers how quiet the girl was that year, and that the school didn't say much, not officially anyway, to the students. "The school probably assumed there would be a ransom, and Ann would be back in a few days," the woman said. "I was scared, and didn't know what to say to Julie. So none of us talked at school about Ann. But my parents talked a lot about it at home." Bev had taken the children with her while she put up the posters, and according to Julie, the children went along to help search the parks, gullies, and ravines for Ann. Presumably, they might have stumbled over their sister's dead body. It was what everyone was looking for, wasn't it? Bev denied that the children helped search, but Julie was adamant that they did, and that it added to their trauma. Of course, Bev didn't drive, so where she went, the children almost always went. Bev and Don didn't believe in babysitters except for Bev's mother, Marie.

Julie was terrified to turn eight years old, but she did on February 28, 1962. She was now the age her sister was when she disappeared. Bev told a newspaper that Julie didn't like being the oldest.

It wouldn't look right for a mother of a missing girl to be pessimistic, so in interview after interview, Bev spoke of having hope. Sometimes she even believed she did. And in articles, Don sounded hopeful. If their relationship with their parish priest was strained, Bev and Don didn't let on. An article mentioned Don quoting Father Godley as having told the family: "She is already with God, if that's the way it is to be."

But Bev was floundering, trying to decide if her Catholic faith was a solace or disappointment. If prior to Ann's disappearance Father Godley didn't see the Burr family in church very often, that would change. Julie's memory of the months after Ann disappeared are of Sundays and how her mother would sit in church, sobbing. "When she was first taken, I thought it was God's will," Bev said. "Later I said, 'That was a stupid thing to say.'" Bev wrestled with what she believed, but regardless, she concluded every prayer with these words to herself: "And bless our Ann."

7
The Birth of the Hunchback

HIS EYES WOULD TURN BLACK. OR HE WOULD suddenly develop a mark on his cheek. Other times he would emit an odor, one more animal than human. From the time Ted was a three-year-old scaring his aunt with knives, to later when teachers, friends, and relatives began to witness his sudden anger, there was a physical metamorphosis that came over him.

Ted's childhood and high school friends witnessed changes in him when he got mad; his normally blue eyes darkened. Ted was quick to rage as a child. If he got angry, he could shove a plate of food in your face. If a fern caught him near an eye during a pretend game of warfare, he would start a fistfight, even with his best friend. He liked to jump out from behind bushes and scare his friends. It wasn't just in the spirit of fun; he experienced a kind of twisted glee if he startled them. On death row, he admitted that as a child, he threw tantrums and urinated in a store to get the attention of his mother. His longtime college girlfriend wrote of a peaceful river rafting trip interrupted when he suddenly lunged at her and shoved her into the water. He couldn't understand why she was upset. He grew up, but in many ways he never matured.

His great-aunt, Virginia Bristol, told of a pleasant evening at a concert in Pennsylvania with Ted, then college-aged. They were standing on a platform waiting for a train when she said Ted suddenly started to verbally ramble; she said that he made no sense and looked crazy and that she was "afraid to be alone with him." Joe Aloi, an investigator for the Florida public defender's office, said that one day when he and Ted were talking, Ted suddenly "became weird." Aloi described how Ted's body and face changed, how there was almost a complete change of personality and how Ted exhibited extreme tension. And Aloi was aware of an odor. He said that was the day he became afraid of Ted.

Journalist Stephen Michaud began to call Ted Bundy "the hunchback" when the Florida prosecutor, while trying Ted for the murder of 12-year-old Kimberly Leach, described what people *think* a criminal is: "a hunchbacked, cross-eyed little monster slithering through the dark, leaving a trail of slime." Michaud, who spent hundreds of hours audio taping interviews with Ted, said he hid behind "a mask of sanity." Like Aloi, and Ted's great-aunt, Michaud witnessed moments of metamorphosis. "When we'd be talking about the murders, he would grab the (tape) recorder and cradle it. There was a white mark on his left cheek, like a scratch. After a while it would fade away." Ted's longtime college girlfriend noticed moments when his eyes looked close together.

During the last 15 years of his life, an army of detectives, psychiatrists, attorneys, journalists and family members of dead girls would struggle to understand the darkness that descended on Ted beginning in his teenage years. In addition to Michaud's "the hunchback," Ted's "problem" would be called "the malignant being" and an "altered state." He would be diagnosed or described as having a life-long personality disorder, bipolar disease (manic depression), dysphasia, abnormal brain chemistry, maladaptive personality structure, affective disorder , and DID (dissociative identity disorder). Ted simply called his talent for hurting others without remorse his "flaw." He learned to compartmentalize, to have "boxes in his head," according to one investigator. He could think of himself as the "good Ted" and the "bad Ted." It was "the other Ted," "the entity," who was responsible for those horrible murders. And yet he would never let his attorneys use "the other Ted" as a defense for his crimes.

Experts debated—are *still* debating—exactly what the early and adolescent influences on Ted were. As a teenager, Ted almost certainly began to show evidence of the manic depression that plagued both his grandparents. It took different forms in them: his grandfather was violent and controlling, his grandmother prone to depression and agoraphobia (and who knows what traits his birth father might have passed on to Ted). One psychiatrist believed that because Ted always bludgeoned his victims, he had most likely been beaten with a stick—by a woman—when he was a child.

As he entered his teenage years, a pattern began to emerge; when he was in the grips of the downside of his depression he lied, he stole, he manipulated others, he felt no empathy and no responsibility for his own actions and—eventually—he killed. Alcohol or marijuana helped him to act on his impulses and act out his fantasies. When he was on a manic upswing, he would move, change colleges, and change majors. Then his moods would drop again, and he couldn't go to classes, would sabotage himself and his relationships, drop out of school, drink, smoke pot, prowl, steal, and kill. He called them his "frenzy episodes," even while continuing to proclaim his innocence.

Dr. Dorothy Lewis, the psychiatrist who worked on Ted's behalf near the end of his life, testified that Ted had "no insight into these wide fluctuations" before she documented his ups and downs. She could chart his mood swings to when he had committed crimes. There would be an upswing of mania that would lead to killings; the depression came after—not over his hurting someone, but over the physical release killing provided him. She says that during his "frenzy episodes" his compulsions would build, and what little impulse control he had lessened. Only killing would quiet his rage.

She saw a metamorphosis, too, which she explained as a kind of a dissociative state similar to a fugue state or a hysterical state. "...These are times when sometimes individuals go off and don't even know who they are for a period of time, and wind up somewhere else in the country," she testified to a

Florida court. "And they don't know how they got there... my guess is there is abnormal brain activity, but we don't, we just don't know what causes them. Certainly there is something episodically going on that is aberrant and abnormal."

An associate of Dr. Lewis' involved in testing Ted concluded that he had experienced "severe early deprivation." And early deprivation is as serious as any other kind of child abuse.

But his parents and half-siblings saw nothing, or said they saw nothing. To his mother, Louise, he would always be the thoughtful young man who never forgot to send flowers on Mother's Day. His half-sister, Linda Bussey, six years younger than Ted and the oldest of Louise and Johnnie's four children, recalls only "a great childhood, super great parents." The man who finally admitted to killing dozens of young women—and hinted of many more—was, according to Bussey, "not the person I knew."

Bussey still lives in Tacoma, near where Louise and Ted first settled and just blocks from the UPS campus and the Burr home. Repeating "it was a great childhood," is all she will say about Ted's early years. She says she never talked with Ted about who his birth father was, and claims she has never given any thought to what made Ted arguably the most famous serial killer in America. Her explanation of their childhood and home life is much like Ted and Louise denying there was anything amiss at his grandparent's house.

Without question, the most complicated relationship of Ted's life was with his mother. For most of his life, Ted Bundy would tell himself—and others—conflicting stories about his parentage. When he confided his illegitimacy to Ann Rule (a friend and co-worker at a crisis hotline in Seattle who was writing a book about the search for a young killer with only a first name, "Ted"), he said he was raised believing that Louise was his sister and that he was a "late baby" born to Samuel and Eleanor Cowell. A college girlfriend, who under the pseudonym Elizabeth Kendall wrote about her six-year long relationship with Ted, stated that he cried when he told her about finding out he was illegitimate.

"Ted told a little different story to everybody. He lied all the time," said Rule. "It was very hard to tell when Ted was being genuine," according to Stephen Michaud, who believes it is "entirely possible" that his grandfather, Samuel Cowell, was Ted's father.

Some heard a story about Ted's cousin taunting him about being illegitimate; some saw him angry and resentful of his mother for the embarrassment of his birth. To others he told a story about how he had "found" his birth certificate, saying "father unknown." Still other close teenage friends say Ted never mentioned his illegitimacy.

"My impression is that Ted felt humiliated by circumstances of his birth. He felt alone in that shame," said his last attorney, Polly Nelson. And Nelson, as well as boyhood friends of Ted's, said he had only a slight relationship with his step-father. "I had the impression that Johnnie didn't exist at all; he ignored him," Nelson said. The circumstances of his birth set the stage for Ted's complicated relationship with Louise. "If she was humiliated when he was born, imagine her humiliation when he was arrested," said Nelson.

There is great sympathy for the people fated to be the parents of Ted Bundy (except from those authors, psychiatrists or investigators who hoped to get Louise Bundy to give them insights into Ted, and found her unhelpful). Sandi Holt, who knew Louise and Johnnie Bundy from Cub Scout outings and as the parents of her brother's friend, said Louise was "very loving, caring and nurturing to Ted. I saw it in her participating in scouting."

But longtime family friends, and some relatives, call the Bundys a secretive family. Ted's cousin, Edna Martin, said "nobody knows" who Ted's father was—and that her parents never knew. "We did hear that rumor" that Ted was born of an incestuous encounter, Martin said. "I think Ted had a real need to find out who he was. He was relieved Johnnie wasn't his father." She calls the Bundys "a close family" and her cousin Ted "a close friend." Like Doug Holt, her brother, John, considered Ted his best friend. Yet, Ted envied the Cowell's lifestyle, the music always present in the house, the foreign sports cars, and the trips to Europe.

Those who got to know the family only after Ted's arrests have strong opinions, too. "I wouldn't call her cold," attorney Polly Nelson said of Louise. "I'd call her controlled. She wasn't a bad person, or a drunk, she was a simple person. She was so overwhelmed that she didn't have anything to give him. He didn't admire her, he had contempt. He was really envious of his half-siblings, how comfortable and easy it was for them."

Stephen Michaud said Ted lied to his parents about his crimes for years and that they believed Ted was innocent— until Michaud arrived in Tacoma with a tape recorder to play them one of Ted's confessions. "His mother was simply another person to use," Michaud said.

8

One Year Later

BEV THREW HERSELF INTO THE BLACKBERRY brambles. Her family thought she was simply working to clear the land near her father's cabins on Fox Island. But she knew what she was doing was a form of atonement. Her arms bled, her hands bled, her legs bled, and she wanted them to. Bev was not one to cry, so maybe the pain, the isolation of the work, the scrapes, and the bleeding, would distract her and give her an outward way to mourn. As Tom Robbins would write, "Nothing, not mushrooms, not ferns, not moss, not melancholy, nothing grew more vigorously, more intractably in the Puget Sound rains than blackberries."

Well, maybe in Bev's case, melancholy might defeat the blackberries. It was one year since Ann had vanished, and the family was back at the place that held many happy family memories, and some imperfect ones, too, if Bev was honest with herself. Photographs taken every summer had nearly the same pose: Mary, Greg, Julie, and Ann, with Barney, the cocker spaniel, lined up, youngest to oldest, left to right. Now there was a vacant space where Ann should be. The blackberry bushes presented an opportunity to Bev. "I thought, this will get my anger and feelings out so I'll do it 'till it's done."

Tacoma police had spent 5,000 man hours looking for Ann. Eight hundred soldiers, volunteers, police officers and Boy Scouts had searched. Police had questioned 1,500 people in just the first 12 days of the investigation and given polygraphs to 200 of them. Detectives had lived in Bev's basement for a month, waiting for a credible ransom demand that never came. Julie was the most troubled by her sister's disappearance. The other children were too young to comprehend what had happened. For five-year-old Greg, it was a bit of a lark. He liked the novelty of the police around their house and announced that he wanted to be a detective when he grew up.

Police departments in 200 cities in the west were urged to be on the lookout for Ann. Bev spent hours at the library, finding the names and addresses of newspapers in the U.S. and Canada. She composed a news release and sent a copy to at least one newspaper in every major city. She had inquiries back from only one or two. Bev carried a stack of the missing poster with Ann's photo wherever she went; police had mailed twenty thousand of them to other law enforcement agencies.

The daily visits from Detectives Ted Strand and Tony Zatkovich had slowed, but the two paid a one-year anniversary visit to Bev and Don, extending their sympathies and letting the family know they were still on the case. The Tacoma and Seattle newspapers ran stories acknowledging the one-year mark and updating the investigation. The headline on one in the Seattle Post-*Intelligencer* read, "Police detectives fear the happy, plump-cheeked child was carried off by a mental or sexual deviate." Another headline read: "Strange Mystery Strengthens Faith of Grieved Parents." In an odd restaging, Bev was photographed tucking Mary, now four years old, into what had been Ann's bed. "Mary Cried the Night Sister Ann Vanished a Year Ago," the caption states. Julie didn't want to stay in the bedroom she had shared with Ann, so she changed rooms, and Mary moved into it. But the illustrations on the wall, the headboard, the lamps, and bedspread and ruffles remained Ann's.

As painful as the newspaper stories were, Bev knew that reminders of Ann's disappearance could prompt leads in the case. Bev, who knew her dream of being a writer had died, still had the journalist's instinct to chronicle everything. She carefully collected the articles and began to paste them in Ann's baby book. Following pages detailing her daughter's first steps, birthdays, and other childhood milestones ("she is aware of strangers," Bev wrote when Ann turned one), there were now clippings about her disappearance. An album created after 1961 was labeled simply "After Ann." Dozens would follow.

By the time Bev was tearing at the blackberry vines, Detectives Strand and Zatkovich had spent hundreds of nights sitting in their car, smoking, and dissecting the Burr case. Their respite was flying lessons and then the purchase of a small plane. They kept it at an airfield in Fife, a small town east of Tacoma. They would fly their families down the

Washington and Oregon coastline. Their years in a patrol car, and then as detectives, had made them "closer than brothers." "You couldn't get any closer," is how Strand's son Ted (the third generation in his family named Ted Strand) describes them.

In 1961, they were in their late 40s and were Tacoma's reigning crime fighters. They had survived the vigilante years, when, convinced that some police and city leaders were taking graft, they led dozens of other policemen on surprise raids of gambling and liquor establishments. They were fired by the city official they had embarrassed. But the town, especially the PTA, the Council of Churches, and the local newspapers, were outraged about the treatment of the police officers and of how the town fathers tolerated vice, all because a certain amount of gambling and prostitution should be expected in a seaport town.

After weeks of hearings packed with "overflow crowds," and the accusation by one of the former vigilantes that the two detectives were themselves on the take, they were reinstated with back pay. Zatkovich and Strand were assigned to what they considered Siberia, a beat in an area of the city so remote that it clearly showed they were in still in disfavor with their supervisors. But they remained popular with the newspaper reporters, who looked for any occasion to write about the two, even their arrest of a trick-or-treater who had vandalized a neighborhood on Halloween. By 1951, Zatkovich had lost his badge three times. Still, he was named Police Chief that year; within three months he had mouthed off to the city council and was sent back to the streets in a patrol car. He never stopped being outspoken, including about women police officers. He said they made him "sick," and in a newspaper interview called them "women bulls."

Strand stood by Zatkovich when his partner accidentally shot and killed a teenage girl as he chased a suspected felon. Because of lingering hard feelings with city government, Zatkovich was charged with second-degree murder. A jury acquitted him, and he was restored to duty, again. The duo seemed to have nine lives.

Strand's four children were older than Zatkovich's two sons, and by 1961, Strand was a grandfather four times over; Zatkovich's sons were at Wilson High School (where they knew a boy named Ted Bundy). The Strands and the Zatkovichs camped together and went on flying trips, but Ted and Tony's friendship was the catalyst for the families socializing. Ted and Tony were each other's yin and yang. Strand was the cool headed one; Zatkovich wasn't.

At their respective homes, the detectives didn't talk about the Burr case; together, it was almost all they could think about. They had never *not* solved a major case. In addition to speaking with the Burrs regularly, the detectives had stayed in touch with the other Donald Burr, the architect, the one who also had a young daughter. He remained convinced that his daughter had been the intended target. After tracing the movements of Burr's first wife, the mother of young Debra Sue Burr, Strand and

Zatkovich had not been able to place Poldi or her husband Emile in the Tacoma area in 1961. There were lots of sightings of their make and model of car—a T-bird convertible with Illinois plates—but the detectives were almost certain that Poldi was in her native Austria in early August, the month Ann disappeared. What they couldn't determine is where she went when she left Vienna on August 19.

Nineteen hundred sixty-two wasn't a summer Bev looked forward to, but neither was any summer. "I never liked summer. Something always goes wrong," she remembered. It was summer, 1942, when Bev's closest friend, along with thousands of other Japanese, was expelled from Tacoma.

Haruye Kawano was one of six Japanese children in Bev's sixth grade class at Central Elementary School; after Central, the girls went on to Jason Lee Junior High School. They had a lot in common; both their fathers owned small grocery stores, they lived just a few blocks from each other, and both girls were ambitious and competitive. "She was always elected president, I was elected vice president. It got to be irritating," Bev joked.

In April, 1942, when the girls were 14 years old, eight thousand Japanese, including Haruye, her parents and her four siblings were sent to a "Jap camp" built in the valley, near Puyallup. It was named Camp Harmony. The Tacoma News Tribune reported that Old Glory "flew proudly" over the camp, and that by summer the "Japs" had made a "cheerful exit," and boarded the train for internment camps at Pinedale, California and Twin Falls, Idaho.

The evacuation was "accomplished on time and without incident." The newspaper boasted that only five "Jap" were left in the city—three were in jail and two were in hospitals. The city would be rid of them as soon as possible.

After several weeks at Camp Harmony, Haruye and her family were sent away. Bev went to the train station to say goodbye to her young friend. She felt helpless as she stood and waved as the train pulled out of Tacoma, and Haruye and her family left a city that didn't want them. Despite the description in the Tacoma News Tribune, it was not a cheerful exit.

A year later it was put before the people of Tacoma: did they want the Japanese to return? A majority said no, and it was early 1945 before they were allowed to resettle in Tacoma. But not all of them came back. Bev learned that her friend eventually became a nurse and lived in Chicago, but they never saw each other again. Bev was not good at making close friends. She would never again try in the same way.

It was summer, 1951, when Bev married Don. They had met as students at the University of Washington. During the war Don served in the Army Air Corps, where he learned accounting and bookkeeping. During one of their many breakups, Don dropped out of college and went to Alaska where he worked as an accountant and played the clarinet and saxophone in a dance band. And then he returned to Seattle and showed up at Bev's door. By then she had graduated from Pacific Lutheran

University in Tacoma and was living in one of her father's cabins on the east side of Fox Island, not far from Honeymoon Bay. She taught at the small school on the island, at what was known as Sylvan, Washington.

Bev's father was not an outdoorsman, but he suspected that the land would be worth something, someday, as the surrounding cities grew. His efforts at owning land and cabins—especially ones that required a boat to get to— were mixed. On one of the family's first outings, the boat began to take on water and nearly sank before the family reached shore. He was relieved when a bridge connecting the island to the mainland was built in 1954.

Bev liked teaching, but found it hard. It was her first experience, and she had four grades in one room at the island school. But her friend Larry M__ was teaching at the same school. It was not a coincidence. Although he was married, M__ was in love with Bev and she knew it. After Don's return from Alaska, Bev agreed to marry Don. But the day before the wedding, Larry made a last appeal to Bev: he would leave his wife and young daughter for her. He begged her not to marry Don. Bev went to her parents, saying she wanted to call off the wedding. "They said I would ruin their lives," Bev remembered. "I should have done what I wanted to do." She was headstrong, but not enough to defy her parents. She often wondered over the years: would she be any happier as the wife of an insurance salesman, which is what Larry became when he left teaching? Would Larry M__ have encouraged her, in ways that Don didn't, to write, to drive, to be fun-loving?

Bev's thoughts on what constituted a successful life were not popular with her parents. "I did not want to get married and raise a bunch of kids but that was not normal; what was normal was to marry and have kids," she would say. But she had "big dreams." She wanted to be a journalist or, as she stated candidly, a "famous writer." When she spoke of her dream, she pantomimed being in the trenches and holding a rifle. She wanted to go where the action was.

Bev and Don were married in her parent's living room on August 6, 1951. Bev knew quickly that it was a mistake, that she and Don were not compatible. "I was really in love with someone else," Bev told Raleigh Burr's second wife, Bonnie Taschler. Ann was born 16 months later.

After Ann disappeared, the police spoke with Larry M__. Bev had included his name on a list of family, friends, neighbors, and acquaintances to be checked out. M__ willingly met with the police at their headquarters and told them he had not had contact with Bev in years. That may, or may not, have been the truth.

Now it was summer again, one year since Ann had vanished. As Bev hacked at the blackberries, she thought of Ann, of what lay ahead. Ann's dog Barney would have to be put to sleep; he was having seizures. In a few days the children would start at a new school. They wouldn't return to Grant, which

Ann had attended. Bev hoped they would be safer at the parish school at St. Patrick's. And Bev planned to put away some of the family photos long-displayed at the brick bungalow on N. 14th Street. The ones with Ann were too heart-wrenching to see every day.

And then there was a subject she planned to bring up to Don. Sometime after Mary was born Don had had a vasectomy (there were rumors that the Catholic Church would soon ease its stand on birth control, but Bev had never been particularly devout, and Don never formally joined the church). So if they were to contemplate filling the void that Ann had left, they would need to adopt. Bev began to think about the possibility. Another blonde-haired baby girl, another chance.

Bev was certain that Ann was dead and that the person responsible was someone the family knew. Don was more optimistic. "He was very quiet; he went to his job every day. He had a lot to do, which is probably good," Bev said. "He didn't quite accept it. I knew different."

9

The Cary Grant of Serial Killers

He practiced posing. He could *appear* scholarly. He could *appear* confident. He could *appear* charming, the all-American boy-next-door. Except the boyishness was really immaturity, and in a few years when he most wanted to impress young women, his posing didn't work. He could only get them if he killed them.

In high school Ted felt that he didn't understand social situations and social cues; within a couple of years he found that he didn't have to understand them—he could pretend. So he did. He gave off a glibness, a charm that was superficial but that many young women, and the state's politicians, thought was brilliance, even genius. There was talk, after he got involved in Republican state politics, that he might be another John Kennedy (a young *Republican* John Kennedy). Political leaders who he drove for, or spied for, or whose parties he attended, treated him like a favorite nephew.

"I became expert at projecting something very different," Ted said later. "That I was busy. It is clear now, I think, that a huge part of my life was hidden from everyone—secret, as it were. It didn't take much effort at all."

Ted was good at over-claiming—exaggerating or fabricating his knowledge, experience and background to impress others. He pretended to be a law student when he was a just a junior at the University of Washington. He took a summer class in Chinese language at Stanford University in order to impress a former girlfriend, but became "extremely depressed" and didn't complete it. He considered a career in architecture, again to impress a girlfriend, but his grades weren't good enough to get into the classes at the University of Washington. He eventually settled on studying psychology.

He couldn't sustain the suave charm that earned him, briefly, the moniker "The Cary Grant of serial killers." In truth, the thing he was best at was undermining himself. He would stay in jobs just a few weeks or months (until he was suspected of stealing, or simply stopped showing up). He dropped in and out of colleges. Most importantly, he sabotaged his various trials by swaggering before juries that were deciding his life or death, and by either trying to represent himself or refusing to cooperate with defense attorneys. He would not plea bargain, even if it would have saved his life.

After graduating from Wilson High School in Tacoma in 1965 (with average grades), Ted lived at home and attended the University of Puget Sound, the campus that he and his mother had lived near when they first arrived in Tacoma, and the campus that was searched for any trace of young Ann Marie Burr. In 1966, after less than a year at UPS and a gap of several months, he transferred to the University of Washington's Asian studies program, first living in a dorm, and then moving to an apartment. Ted later told a psychiatrist that his first years of college focused on his "longing for a beautiful coed."

His mood disorder presented itself by 1967, at the latest. He began to have severe bouts of depression; he would be unable to attend classes, would isolate himself with alcohol and marijuana, and had increasing trouble controlling his fantasies. When the mania aspect of his bi-polar disease kicked in, he got involved in politics, felt "charismatic," "oozed sincerity," according to one admirer, changed majors, and for several years maintained a seemingly normal relationship with a divorcee with a young child.

His mother, Louise, thought Ted's "trouble" (meaning the murders of at least 30 women and possibly dozens more) began when Ted was rejected by a girlfriend. They met in the fall of 1966, Ted's first term at the University of Washington. Referred to as "Stephanie," "Marjorie," "Susan," or "Diane," (all pseudonyms) in books about Ted, she was pretty, with long hair parted in the middle and from a California family with money. She was "wealthy, poised and worldly," everything Ted wasn't. She eventually broke things off with Ted; later, she told investigators that she had tired of his games (including sneaking up on her and trying to frighten her) and had concluded that his boyishness was really immaturity. A couple of years later, when he had worked on his more refined persona, he re-met "Stephanie." They became close again; in fact, she thought they were engaged. And then he suddenly dropped her, with no explanation. It had been a ruse, a game, just like the ones he and Doug Holt used to play on friends in Tacoma. It was one of his "getting over" games, tricking her to get even for the heartache she had caused him.

For years, people would theorize that the young women he murdered—many with long hair, parted in the middle—were stand-ins for "Stephanie" or even his mother. (Later, Ted said that he wasn't pursing a "stereotype" so much as a "certain class" of woman.) If his first murders were committed in 1974 (and not in the 1960s, as many believe), then they began just a month after he played his trick on "Stephanie." Most detectives and psychiatrists who studied Ted discount the possibility that he was "killing," over and over, the girl who had first rejected him. Thousands of young women at the University of Washington had long hair parted in the middle, were pretty, and lived in sororities. One of them was Julie Burr, who not only was at UW when Ted was, but often visited Lake Sammamish, the scene of one of Ted's most infamous crimes. Their paths may have very well have crossed.

Ted's cousin, Edna Cowell, also at UW, introduced him to all her friends; they all had long hair parted in the middle. In fact, a friend of Edna's was a close friend of Ted's first known victim, Lynda Ann Healy. Like Ted, Healy was a psychology major at UW, and they reportedly had classes together. One night, Edna's friend had a date to meet up with Healy; she never showed up. She had been abducted that morning, January, 31, 1974, from her basement apartment near UW. Her remains, and the remains of three other victims, were found on Taylor Mountain, east of Seattle, in March, 1975.

In the fall of 1969, Ted met Elizabeth Kendall in a bar near campus. Liz was 24 years old and divorced, with a two-year-old daughter. Liz and Ted dated for five years, until 1974, when he moved to Utah for another try at law school (after dropping out of UPS). During Ted and Liz's relationship, at least 10 young women disappeared in the Pacific Northwest. Most were students on college campuses in Oregon and Washington. When Ted moved to Utah to attend law school, the killings mysteriously stopped in the Northwest and began in Utah and Colorado. Liz began to suspect that her boyfriend could be the mysterious "Ted" police were looking for.

Ted's cousin, Edna, got to know Liz, but they were never close, probably because of Liz's insecurities. "Ted and I were good friends, and she'd be incredibly jealous, insecure, super-needy," according to Edna. In her defense, it was not easy to be Ted's girlfriend. She experienced firsthand Ted's moodiness, disappearances, secrets, and games. Like the others, she didn't understand his love of startling people. There were indications that Ted was hiding parts of his life. As police looked for a young man with a cast on his arm or crutches, who tried to lure women to his car by asking them for help with his books or a sailboat, (often using a quasi-British accent), Liz found plaster of Paris and crutches in

Ted's apartment, and a hatchet under the seat of his car.

In a memoir of her life with Ted, Liz Kendall wrote that twice, when they were having sex, Ted deliberately put his arm on her windpipe, choking her. At least one of those times Ted went into a trance, and she had trouble getting him to let go. Then, on the Fourth of July weekend, 1974, the two were floating down the Yakima River. Liz was perched on the edge of the rubber raft when suddenly he "lunged" at her, put his hands on her shoulders, and pushed her into the river.

As she struggled in the icy water and managed to pull herself back into the raft, he was expressionless, she wrote. The incident happened just days before one of Ted's most horrific crimes, the murders of two young women he lured separately from Lake Sammamish State Park on July 14, 1974. That's when police finally had a name for the man they were looking for. There were several women whose lives were saved that day because they declined to help the man who said his name was "Ted."

But Liz saw evidence of the "other" Ted, too, the one that warned her to not walk in a park late at night, the one who brought home stray animals, the one who watched cartoons and had tickle fights with her young daughter. The one who comforted her when she found herself pregnant with his baby, and when they agreed to an abortion. Ted even became a Mormon, because Liz was.

One day while shopping together at a mall in north Seattle, Ted suddenly shoved a package he was carrying at Liz and took off running. She heard a woman with two young children scream and point at a man who had grabbed her purse. Ted caught the purse-snatcher and turned him over to security. Eventually, Liz Kendall called police with her suspicions that *her* Ted was the Ted they were looking for. More than once she was told he had been checked out and eliminated as a suspect.

During his college years Ted stepped up his nighttime activities. He would later tell police in Florida that he felt "most alive at night," and he would refer to himself as a "vampire." According to an FBI report compiled after his execution, Ted "was involved in voyeuristic activities throughout his life and actually studied his victims without their knowledge through surveillance and occasional clandestine entry of their residences." He later admitted to conducting "dry runs," picking up a woman and "releasing her unharmed to test his skills." His voyeurism turned into more dangerous fantasies in 1973, when he bought his first Volkswagen, a tan, 1968 model, for four hundred dollars. (In 1975 he sold that VW and bought a newer one.)

The million dollar question is: when did Ted's behavior evolve from dry runs to murder? To the end of his life, Ted Bundy would not reveal when he committed his first murder. Some, including author Ann Rule, think Ann Marie Burr may have been his first victim.

Ted was a paid work-study student and Rule, a former police officer who had started her career as a writer, was a volunteer at a Seattle crisis center telephone hotline. Forced to leave police work because of her eyesight, she sometimes wrote reports for police departments, summarizing evidence on cases. And she began to sell magazine articles to detective magazines, like the ones Ted used to read. Years later, Ted denied having anything to do with the disappearance of Ann Marie Burr because it was "close to home" and because Ann was so young, according to Ann Rule. But serial killers frequently won't admit to killing children; it is the ultimate stigma, and one other inmates are unforgiving of. Bob Keppel, who helped investigate the "Ted" murders as a King County detective, came to know Ted Bundy well. When Keppel asked Ted about Ann Marie Burr, "He did not want to talk about this case, and every denial he made was unconvincing," Keppel wrote.

Ted claimed he committed his first murder in May, 1973, when he picked up a hitchhiker near Olympia, Washington. The FBI could never confirm that, and never found a body that matched Ted's confession.

But the Ted Bundy legend begins earlier. On June 23, 1966, two stewardesses, Lonnie Trumbull and Lisa Wick, both 20 years old, were attacked in the apartment they shared on the east side of Seattle's Queen Anne Hill. They were found the next morning by their third roommate, who had stayed with another stewardess that night. Trumbull was bludgeoned to death but Wick, badly injured and comatose for days, survived. Doctors said she might have died if she hadn't been sleeping on curlers; they bore some of the brunt of the bludgeoning.

The three roommates, all from Portland, had graduated from the United Airlines training school in Chicago six weeks before the attack. While Wick was recuperating from brain surgery, police showed her a photo of Richard Speck, by then a suspect in the killing of eight student nurses in Chicago on July 14, 1966; she didn't think it was Speck. (Speck was convicted and sentenced to death; he died in prison in 1991 at age 50 of a heart attack.) About three weeks after the Seattle attack, the newspapers reported that Wick had been able to give the police a description of the man who killed her roommate and assaulted her. She described him as a slender blonde man, about 30 years old. One newspaper gave a few other details: it said he had a receding hairline and a light complexion, was around five feet, nine inches tall and weighed about 165 pounds.

Ted was 19 years old the summer of 1966. He was five feet, ten inches, weighed about 165 lbs., and had thick, curly brown hair. (When his killing spree was in high gear, he was good at changing his appearance; he would part his hair on the other side, wear a fake moustache, or change his posture. And he knew how to alter the impression he made, whether wearing his tennis whites to a park in the summer, or a suit and bowtie in court.) He was in the midst of moving from Tacoma to Seattle, where he would attend the University of Washington.

According to an FBI chronology of his life, he attended the University of Puget Sound until April, 1966, and was not at the UW until September of that year. He didn't appear to have a job that summer.

In early 1968, Ted dropped out of the UW, and traveled. He went to San Francisco, Denver, and Aspen, where he skied. He also went to Philadelphia and presumably saw his grandparents. When he returned to Seattle, he worked from April, 1968, until July, 1968, at a Safeway grocery store in the neighborhood where Lonnie Turnbull and Lisa Wick were attacked. Besides that coincidence and the fact that they were beaten with a piece of wood—a weapon Ted often used—there is no evidence that it was his first crime. A favorite suspect of the Seattle police was the apartment owner's son, who later committed suicide; a newspaper article about the murder was found in his belongings. But Ann Rule says Lisa Wick wrote to her, saying she believes Ted Bundy was their assailant, and he remains a suspect in the minds of some long-retired police officers.

Ted went east again, in January, 1969, and enrolled at Temple University in Philadelphia. He was there just one semester. On the way east he stopped to visit his cousins, the Cowells, in Fayetteville, Arkansas. Jack Cowell, the UPS music professor Ted looked up to, had received his doctorate at the University of Washington in 1966, then joined the faculty at the University of Arkansas.

Ted's cousin Edna remembers his stop in Fayetteville. "He asked my parents for money. I don't remember if they gave him any," she said. Ted stayed a few days, Edna took him out for a meal, to a 1950s-style drive-in, and then he continued his trip east. The Cowells moved back to the northwest in 1985, although Edna returned to Seattle in 1970 to attend the University of Washington.

There's a danger in romanticizing Ted's trips east, in 1968 and 1969. He is depicted as looking for answers as to who he was and who his father was. He may have traveled to Vermont, he may have visited The Elizabeth Lund Home for Unwed Mothers in Burlington, he may have seen his birth certificate for the first time, he may have finally learned once and for all that he was illegitimate and that the woman he once thought his sister was actually his mother. Or not. He told so many different people so many different stories; he could shrug off his illegitimacy, or cry in the laps of girlfriends.

One thing Ted did for sure in 1969: he went into New York City, a lot. He told his attorney, Polly Nelson, and psychiatrist, Dr. Dorothy Otnow Lewis, that he often took the train from Philadelphia to New York City. "I remember coming into New York this time, this very first time I was going to try something, you know, of course it was very... amateurish... I bought a fake mustache and bought hair stuff—some hair dye. I registered in some seedy hotel-motel under a false name and all these things. I had this horribly inept plan in mind, and I wasn't sure exactly where it was going to go." His plan, he said, was... "following some woman in some hotel to her room and rushing in on her and doing... I wasn't sure what... I think sexually assaulting her."

This is likely the visit east when his great-aunt, Virginia Bristol, after attending a concert with Ted, suddenly felt frightened as they stood on a platform waiting for a train. She said Ted started to verbally ramble, that he looked crazy, and she was afraid to be alone with him.

On Memorial Day, 1969, just as Ted prepared to leave Pennsylvania and head west again, he made a stop at the New Jersey shore. That weekend, a parkway maintenance worker discovered the bodies of two young women in underbrush off the Garden State Parkway. Nineteen-year-olds Susan Davis and Elizabeth Perry had spent the holiday weekend like thousands of other young people, staying at a rooming house in Ocean City, going to the boardwalk and beach, and hitting the clubs. They were found stabbed to death three days after they were expected home. Before he was executed, Ted did a series of interviews with a court-approved forensic psychiatrist, Dr. Art Norman. Norman says that Ted—speaking in the third person, which he did a lot of before he died—claimed responsibility for the "Co-Ed Murders." Or did he? Stabbing was not his modus operandi: bludgeoning was.

Ted told Dr. Lewis, in recorded interviews, that a visit to Ocean City in 1969 was the first time he... "...approached a victim, spoke to her, tried to abduct her, and she escaped." The experience left Ted with the realization of how "inept" he was. "Let's say, this first incident in '69," he told Dr. Lewis. "It was two years later before I did another one, and then six months later before I tried another one, and then finally the first (murder)."

The Ocean City murders were never solved, and never definitely linked to Ted. It is just one of thousands of times Ted would contradict himself. Although he implicated himself in the 1969 New Jersey murders, he also claimed that he first murdered in 1973.

That was about the time Ted's name and photo first appeared in the *Seattle Times.* Shortly after Ted graduated from the University of Washington in 1972, he went to work for the re-election campaign of Governor Dan Evans. Evans was challenged by former Washington governor, Democrat Albert D. Rosellini. During the last weeks of the campaign, reporters noticed a handsome young man who appeared at all of Rosellini's speeches and appearances. Finally, Richard W. Larsen of the *Seattle Times* asked the young man who he was. He said his name was Ted Bundy and he was a graduate student working on a thesis in political science. Eventually, another reporter put two-and-two together and realized that Ted was spying on Rosellini for the Evans campaign. It created a minor controversy, but it was nothing like the dirty tricks that campaigns had pulled before. Ted had impressed Republican party leaders, Larsen did a story about him for the paper, and a friendship was born. Governor Evans wrote a letter on Ted's behalf to the University of Utah law school. Ted was accepted.

Like Ann Rule, Larsen found himself good friends with the man who would soon become the nation's most famous serial killer.

Between 1974 (possibly earlier) and 1978, Ted Bundy killed dozens of young women and girls. Many were students at colleges in the Pacific Northwest. The FBI believed Ted planned and visited some locations before his murders. Susan Rancourt, a student at Central Washington University in Ellensburg, may be an example. She vanished April 17, 1974, within days of a visit Ted paid to his former high school friend, Jerry Bullat, who was attending the college at the time.

His cousin, Edna Martin remembers when she first heard of his first arrest, in 1975. She was working on a crab boat out of Dutch Harbor, Alaska, when the captain called her to the bridge. There was a phone call for her from her brother, telling her that Ted had been arrested in Salt Lake City. They had known, of course, that police in Washington were looking for a man who said his name was "Ted," who drove a tan VW, and who was a suspect in the murders of young women. Now, in Utah, where he was attending law school, Ted had been stopped for attempting to evade police and found with a car full of burglary tools. He was released, but rearrested several weeks later for aggravated kidnapping and attempted criminal homicide.

Martin says she felt "fractured." She left the crab boat and went to see him in Seattle. He was out on bail and visiting the city. He returned to Utah for trial, and by the time he was convicted on those charges, the evidence linking him to dozens of killings had added up. Her parents were "shocked and appalled and sick at heart," Martin said.

Legions of young women would write to Ted in prison; dozens would proposition him. They only saw the Ted who might have become the lawyer, the politician, the smart husband. They saw the handsome young man, sometimes in a suit and bowtie, standing trial. Somehow, lost in the fascination that was the life and crimes of Ted Bundy, is just how horrific his crimes were. He bludgeoned his victims with a crowbar or a piece of wood; he strangled them while raping them; he used metal bed frames, sticks, and ice picks to rip up their vaginas and anuses; he buried them, but kept some of their heads (one time he had as many as four in his apartment). He burned some of the skulls in Liz's fireplace. Sometimes he would return to the site where he disposed of their bodies and wash their hair and put makeup on them. He was only sexually interested in his victims when they were semiconscious, unconscious, or dead. But he didn't just have sex with dead girls. He had sex with decomposing bodies.

The FBI called him "organized." He planned. He preselected the sites where he would dispose of the bodies; he did "discreet research" on his victims; he had his tools conveniently handy; and he planned every moment, from assault, to evidence disposal, to his alibi. It is probably why he left no evidence behind, except for a bite mark on one of his last victims. A few murders were random. If he felt an "urge" to kill, he would pick up a hitchhiker. Some have never been identified because Ted never knew their names and couldn't pinpoint the disposal sites.

Ted returned to nearly all of his crime scenes, sometimes to move or better hide bodies or clothing, sometimes to remove the heads of his victims with a hacksaw. (In fact, he pointed out to the police that they might have caught him if they had staked out sites after finding a body, since he always returned.) Many of his assaults were outdoors, but in Utah he took his victims back to his apartment, where, according to the FBI, he reenacted scenarios depicted on the covers of detective magazines. Like other serial killers, he "improved" as he progressed. According to the FBI, he became "more sophisticated" until the end, when the stress of being a fugitive (after escaping from jail in Glenwood Springs, Colorado) made him impulsive and disorganized. When that occurred, he changed from the "Cary Grant of serial killers," to, as he described himself to Florida police, "...the most cold-blooded son-of-a-bitch you'll ever meet."

10

Life Without Ann

"ADOPTED GIRL HELPS TO FILL ACHING VOID," said the headline in the Tacoma News Tribune. In the summer of 1963, two years after Ann disappeared, the Burrs adopted a baby girl. Bev probably contacted the newspapers herself. It seemed like a happy ending, or as close to one as the Burrs would have. But Bev also had another reason for publicizing the adoption.

In newspaper photographs, Bev and the children (Julie, now nine; Greg, seven; and Mary, now five), show off the new baby. She was blonde and brown-eyed, and the article said that the baby's... "cries, laughter, and hiccups are a welcome addition to the household."

As the Seattle Post-*Intelligencer* reported on July 18, 1963.

> *"No one can ever take the place of Ann Marie in our hearts," said Mrs. Donald Burr yesterday, as she presented publicly for the first time the new baby girl she and her husband recently adopted. The new baby, Laura Gayle, about seven months, woke up smiling. She seemed pure sunshine in the house at 3009 N. 14th St., Tacoma, where for nearly two years*

now there have been heavy mists of sadness and worry."

When a reporter noticed that there were only pictures of Julie, Greg, and Mary on the walls, Bev, "suppressing a sob," went to another room and brought out Ann's picture, explaining.

"I had to take it down and put it in the other room because I just couldn't take it any more looking at the four of them together."

The story went on to explain how Bev felt that adopting a baby "perhaps would help the whole family." She and Don had applied to an agency, and then one day, received a phone call.

"We didn't know if it was a boy or a girl until we went down and got her," Mrs. Burr recalled yesterday. "When we got there they said, 'Oh, does it make any difference if it's a boy or a girl?' and we said, 'No,' and when they said 'It's a girl,' I think I was glad.

"Each day we pray for little Ann, but there is always an emptiness as there was that first night, as though there will be no answer this time. Not like other prayers, when one feels God is listening."

For Bev, sharing news of the adoption was another opportunity to try and find Ann.

"In our hearts, we wish the whole world could stop just a moment and look next door to see if Ann is there."

Bev was quoted as calling Laura "a perfect baby." She would grow up to be the least-troubled of Bev's children.

Just after Bev and Don adopted Laura, the nation's most famous Catholic visited Tacoma. It was the last stop on John Kennedy's cross-country tour "to save America's heritage." Kennedy delivered "a short, impassioned address" on preserving natural resources to 25,000 people crowded into Cheney Stadium (where searchers had looked for Ann's body two years before when it was a construction site). Bev—who was still trying to decide if her Catholic faith was a solace or not—followed the president's visit closely. Two months later, he was assassinated.

Six years to the month after Ann disappeared, the Burrs finally moved. "There was a vacant spot at the dinner table, and Laura filled that," Bev explained. But the home she had once thought of as her "dream house" had become a daily nightmare. "I thought we had to stay there in case Ann tried to reach us," Bev said of the house on North 14th Street, with the window someone had presumably climbed through, the front door Ann had presumably left from, and Ann's bedroom, paintings, books, and dolls. It was too painful for Bev to bear. Anytime an update appeared in the newspapers (including the happy news of the adoption), the line of cars driving slowly past the house resumed. For years, when Bev ran into the family that bought the bungalow on North 14th, she would apologize. She knew the traffic never stopped.

The Burrs moved to a large colonial home on North 28th in Tacoma. It had a huge yard and garden to occupy Bev, and a view of Commencement Bay. Bev called the police department to notify them of the new address; she also told police they were hoping to keep the same telephone number, in case Ann might call. Many of Ann's belongings, including the jumper she never got to wear to her first day of third grade, and two of her dolls, made the move to North 28th.

The newspapers showed Bev, Greg, and Laura unpacking in their new home. "Peace of Mind In Offing?" the headline speculated. The story informed readers that the move was the first for the family since Anne [*sic*] Marie disappeared and reminded them that it remained "one of Tacoma's most noted unsolved cases." In later years Don and Bev would almost always be out of the country when August rolled around.

The Bundy family moved, too. Ted graduated from Woodrow Wilson High School in 1965, and that year Johnnie, Louise, their four children, and Ted left the house on Skyline, where Ted and Doug Holt's mischievous childhood included animal abuse and an intricate series of tricks on their friends. The Bundy's returned to North Tacoma, to North 20th Street, back to the neighborhood near the University of Puget Sound campus where Louise and Ted had lived with her great-uncle, back to within blocks of both of the Burr homes. Sandi Holt, her brother, Doug, and their mother moved too—to Puyallup, east of Tacoma—to get away from Sandi's father.

Adopting Laura and moving out of the house Ann had vanished from did not heal the long-standing problems in Bev and Don's marriage. In photographs there is no affection shown between Don and Bev, at any stage in their lives. And it wasn't that the passion was private, like it is with some couples. There was no heat that took place away from cameras. Bev just didn't feel that way about Don. His verbal cruelty to her and his controlling ways had quickly taken a toll. He could be mean to Bev, even in front of family. One Mother's Day he ordered Bev, in front of the children, to sit in a chair and not move. He insisted Bev always wear a dress, and she wasn't allowed to talk to the mailman. After one abbreviated driving lesson (cut short when Bev, behind the wheel of a new Packard, put it in gear, stepped on the gas, and drove off an embankment and onto a highway), Don decided once and for all Bev would never, ever be permitted to learn to drive a car. Don was "a loving father, but controlling and near-abusive," Julie explained, years later. Yet, "he loved her dearly."

Bev thought Don was jealous of her college education and writing aspirations. "He didn't like me to do anything original," she said. But, "he would do anything for his kids." In that they were united. The loss of a child destroys many marriages, but after Ann vanished and Mary began to have mental health issues, Bev and Don were stronger together than they would have been apart. "You hear so much—it breaks up a marriage, there is finger-pointing," said Don's brother, Raleigh. "I never heard that. They both loved the children and they held it together."

Maybe they weren't outwardly loving to each other, but their children always knew their parents would do anything for them, sometimes to the detriment of the other siblings.

Still, there was Don's bullying. "There was such tension between Bev and Don," said Bonnie Taschler, who married Raleigh in the late 1970s. "Don would say 'Just be quiet, Bev,' or, 'Beverly, I am talking,' and he would raise a finger at her. He was incredibly jealous. If Bev wore shorts (even while gardening)," he would become upset. "We got along because I gave in," Bev said. That may be, but those who loved her, including daughter Julie, and Raleigh Burr and Bonnie Taschler, speak of her stubbornness and headstrong nature that could make it hard to love Bev. And Bev's relationship with Julie became strained. "Every time Bev looked at Julie, she wanted to see Ann," explained Bonnie.

"The marriage was a big mistake," Bev said late in her life. "I could have stormed out, but the children needed me."

Despite their differences, in every newspaper article about Ann and nearly every photograph, there's Don, in a shirt and tie instead of his customary work clothes. Many years after Ann's disappearance, Don continued to call the police department with a tip or a hunch. "He is still obsessed with his daughter's disappearance," whoever took the call would write in the on-going police report. Bev and Don were united in their fierce loyalty to their children. It would be tested again, especially as Mary—the last person to see

Ann, except for her abductor—became a teenager and young adult.

Don was mimicking behavior he had observed as a child. Don and Raleigh's father, Marion (called Frank), was controlling and a "womanizer," according to Raleigh. At least once, Frank left his family to live with another woman. He had been a logger and commercial fisherman in Oregon. When he got the idea of forming his own company, Frank was in trouble financially. Don proposed that they be partners and sent his father five thousand dollars. Soon after their marriage, Don and Bev joined Frank in Oregon. "Dad was the experience, Don was the energy and the muscle," Raleigh said. Later, Frank claimed he owned 51 percent of the company to Don's 49 percent, giving him the right to sell the logging operation without telling Don. There was bad blood between father and son for the rest of their lives.

Raleigh was just 13 or 14 years old when he spent the summer logging with his father and Don. He babysat for Ann, who was born December 14, 1952, in Crescent City, California, the hospital nearest to the base of their logging operation. In the summer, Bev, Don, and Ann, as well as Raleigh and his father, all lived in tents in the woods (they called it "tenting in"). In the winter, Don and Bev and the baby lived in a house in Don's hometown of Grants Pass, or in Brookings, Oregon, on the southern Oregon coast. A logging town since the turn of the century, Brookings had a moment of fame in 1942 when it became the first site in the continental U.S. to be bombed in wartime.

It is still difficult for Raleigh to reconcile the Don he knew and loved, with the Don who berated Bev from the early days of their marriage. "Don was my brother, mentor, and friend," Raleigh said. "He was more my father than my dad was."

It wasn't just Bev and Don who had an awkward physical intimacy. "Don and I would hug, but Bev would shake my hand," explained Raleigh, her brother-in-law more than 50 years. While affectionate with her children, Bev may have learned her physical detachment from her mother. "I never saw Marie touch or hug Bev," said Bonnie. Marie and Bev "didn't like each other," daughter Julie explained. For one thing, "Marie would pit her grandchildren against Bev," according to Julie. Yet Bev and her mother had something in common when each was young. Bev's parents had married when Marie was a teenager and Roy was much older. In an essay that Bev wrote in college, she remembers how frustrating it was for her mother to be young, curious, and enthusiastic, but tied down.

Although Bev and Marie were never close, things improved a little when the children gained a new grandfather. Bev's father, Roy, died in 1956. In 1962, one year after Ann vanished, Marie met Roy's cousin, George Voigt, when he came west to visit the Seattle World's Fair. George had never married, but he and Marie hit it off—he moved out from Chicago; they married and had 20 happy years before George died. He was the only grandfather Bev's children really remembered. “He had no sense of humor; we used to remark on that,” Bev said of George, “but he was a very kind man.” So Marie, who had been only 16 years old when she had married 31-year-old Roy Leach, commenced with what would surely be the best years of her life. Bev had always known that she and her brother Jerry were poor substitutes for Buddy, the first son who had died young. But Bev's children had a new grandfather to dote on them, and George somehow balanced Marie in Bev's life.

Detectives Tony Zatkovich and Ted Strand continued to work every day on the Ann Burr case. In 1963, Zatkovich was quoted in *The Oregonian* as saying police had a clue that they had never disclosed to the public, a common practice to help police sort real leads from false ones. “We haven’t had an opportunity to develop it yet,” he said. Was it the teenage-sized footprint found on the garden bench, or the red thread caught on the window jam, neither of which appeared in news coverage of the time? Did Ann's abductor leave something behind? A hair, saliva or blood? It would be decades before DNA could help match perpetrators with crime scenes.

The detectives decided to take a closer look at some of Don's relatives. Two months after Zatkovich's quote to *The Oregonian*, he and Ted Strand traveled to Yakima, southeast of Mount Rainier, to speak with a nephew of Don's. Larry C__, the son of Don's sister, was 20 years old (18 when Ann vanished). He already had a notorious reputation in the family. Bev had suggested that the detectives talk to Larry about Ann's disappearance; after all, he had already allegedly molested a young family member. Strand and Zatkovich caught up with him at his job at the Boise-Cascade Lumber Co. and took him to the Yakima Police Department to interrogate him. Larry admitted he knew the Burr children well and the layout of the Burr home. The families were often together on holidays. In 1960 and 61, he had been a high school student in Aberdeen, on the south Washington coast, about 80 miles west of Tacoma. He went back and forth to Tacoma with his grandparents, Don's mother and father, for holidays and family gatherings. His alibi for the night Ann Burr disappeared was that he was in California visiting family. When asked about the story in the family that he had molested a young relative, he broke down crying and told police that the story had been fabricated by Raleigh Burr's wife at the time, Sharon. He offered to take a polygraph to prove he had nothing to do with his young cousin's disappearance, but there is no evidence he ever did. According to his family, as an adult, Larry C__ sexually abused his own children and eventually a court order barred him from seeing them. His own mother said of him, "He'll always be in my heart, but not my life." There were other family members with sordid pasts. (As one relative said, "There's been a lot of sexual abuse in this family".) In 1959, a first cousin of Don and Raleigh's was questioned when a young woman was found raped and murdered near Centralia, south of Tacoma. The man's car had broken down near the crime scene. Tacoma police talked to him about the abduction of Ann Marie Burr but he had an alibi; employment records showed he was at work that day, on the "green chain" in the peeling plant at the Allen Logging Company near Forks, Washington. On August 30 and 31 he had worked eight-and-a-half hour shifts beginning at 7 a.m. each day. Another cousin, who police described as "a queer," had been arrested more than once on morals charges. He agreed to a polygraph examination but claimed he had never been to the Burr home or even met Bev and the children. Other relatives had serious money troubles.

Since the Burrs always kept the same phone number, they received more than their share of crank calls over the years. Sometimes Bev was embarrassed to report the incidents to police. On February 20, 1964, she received a call from a man she described as "young, using very good and precise English, no stammering or stuttering, no accent," who said Ann was living with a family in the Phoenix area. He said he would tell her more if Bev undressed for him. Bev was reluctant to share the "embarrassing" details of the man's proposition with the police, but she did. They installed recording equipment in the house again, and two weeks later Detectives Strand and Zatkovich arrested a 17-year-old at Wilson High School (where Ted Bundy was a junior in high school). He admitted making the call to Bev, and said he had no more information about Ann than he had read in the newspapers. He finally confessed to making at least 150 obscene phone calls to women in the previous two or three years. He told police he didn't receive "any particular sexual gratification from the phone calls... he did say it made him warm and sweatty [*sic*]."

Bev called the detectives to complain about their neighbor, Ann's teenage friend Robert Bruzas. Bev said he was spending a lot of time in a car, sitting outside on their street. The police checked it out and most likely told Bev that he was just listening to music on the car radio. They had never found proof to tie him to Ann's disappearance, despite his failing his first polygraph test.

A girl with amnesia was found in Omaha, Nebraska; it wasn't Ann. Two boys found a bottle with a note inside, saying Ann was being held prisoner by bank robbers. Ann's name was found carved on a sandstone cliff at a roadside picnic area southwest of Tacoma, on the way to the Washington coast. Several years after Ann disappeared Bev received an envelope—empty—addressed to their new house on North 28th Street. Bev took the envelope to police, along with one of Ann's school books and begged them to compare the handwriting. Someone in the department studied the envelope and the books and concluded there was no way to tell if it was the writing of the same person, as a child and as a teenager. The books were returned to Bev.

The sense of frustration and disappointment the police faced was evident in the rare emotional comment included in the police report. "It appears that this is just another dead end in the numerous leads we have been receiving on the Ann Burr case," one officer wrote.

Then, suddenly, there were two very real suspects in Ann Marie Burr's disappearance. The story was familiar. On a summer day in Tacoma, a young girl with golden hair went missing. The newspaper caption on her photo read: Another Ann Marie?

For a week in the summer of 1964 Tacoma held its breath again. Ten-year-old Gay Lynn Stewart was "strangely missing" from her home on South Melrose Street. Her relatives and "school chums" did not know where she was. She had last been seen wearing a light blue blouse and cut-off jeans and blue tennis shoes. The story of the missing girl never did get the coverage Ann Marie did, maybe because Gay Lynn seemed a little too worldly for her age. While the police were fearful about parallels to the Burr case, Gay Lynn's parents, Mr. and Mrs. Glenn Stewart, told police that their daughter is a "very intelligent girl and usually entirely capable of taking care of herself." They admitted she had once run away and had been found at the home of a relative. The oldest of six children, Gay Lynn had left home this time "after a minor tiff for which she feared a reprimand," according to the Tacoma News Tribune.

Just like Ann, Gay Lynn was fond of the Point Defiance Park area. In fact, she was standing in the Funland amusement area when she struck up a conversation with a man who said his name was Bob Brown. The two took in a movie at the Fife Drive-In Theater, and then Bob Brown asked her if she would like to take a ride to Spokane.

If the Burr case was, and still is, the coldest case in the Tacoma Police Department files, the Stewart case is one of the oddest. For three days, Gay Lynn

Stewart rode around the Pacific Northwest in a brand new Buick Electra convertible with the man who called himself Bob Brown. He kept a small caliber handgun tucked away in the glove compartment. They ate their meals in restaurants, Gay Lynn got a haircut, and when Bob Brown dropped her off in Tacoma three days later, she also had a new dress, a new pair of shoes and socks, and $15 in her pocket.

After a clerk at Carl's Market & Freezers at 1433 South 56th recognized her and called police, the girl denied her identity and "tartly" told officers, "No—my name is Mickey Anderson." The child was taken to police headquarters where she was questioned before being allowed a brief private meeting with her parents, summoned from their home. They were seen crying as they left police headquarters. Gay Lynn was taken to Remann Detention Hall, where children in custody were housed. She was, in fact, reluctant to return home, according to police. They described her as "dazed" by her trip. Two weeks later, she was still at the detention hall, "for her own protection," police explained. They presumably meant because Bob Brown had not yet been found.

While Gay Lynn told police she and the man had slept in his car, the still unidentified and still on-the-run man was charged with carnal knowledge, as well as kidnapping and flight to avoid prosecution. Gay Lynn helped the police with a composite sketch that was distributed to law enforcement agencies. He must have been known to Spokane police, because they had a mug shot of him they shared with their

Tacoma colleagues. Now, they had a name: he was 48-year-old Ralph Everett Larkee, an automotive parts salesman based in Spokane. Since Larkee and his new Buick convertible had taken Gay Lynn into multiple states, the FBI joined the search.

Two months after his trip with Gay Lynn Stewart, Larkee was found living in a Portland apartment house under the name Paul Lindley. On September 9, 1964, FBI agents knocked on the door and identified themselves. They heard a gunshot and found Larkee had put the small caliber pistol in his mouth and fired. Larkee was in critical condition for six months and never awoke from a coma. He died March 31, 1965, before Tacoma police had a chance to ask him if he had taken another young girl, Ann Marie Burr, for a ride in a convertible.

Richard Raymond McLish loved cars, too. Plymouths, Fords, Dodge Darts. They would be his downfall in his long, but minor, criminal career. He was good at stealing cars, and good at escaping from the Oklahoma State Penitentiary, but he wasn't good at staying out of prison. Nicknamed "Mountain Red" because he was tall and handsome, with blue eyes and curly red hair and freckles, McLish was a member of Oklahoma's Chickasaw Nation. Left motherless at age two, by age 13 McLish had quit school and lied his way into the U.S. Army. He received a dishonorable discharge at age 17—for stealing a car. The state of Oklahoma never knew what to do with McLish; it tested his IQ twice and came up with wildly different numbers, 76 and 107. He was likeable and easygoing and almost no trouble as an inmate. Only twice did his behavior inside lengthen his stay: once when he was found with homemade beer, and the second time when he stole a prison truck and escaped. He never learned a trade. When he wasn't in prison he worked as a hospital attendant, a cook, a meat packer, or in a salvage yard.

In the summer of 1961, McLish, his wife Juanita, and their three young children were picking beans and living in a shack on a farm in Oregon's Willamette Valley. He was friendly with another family on the farm, David and Enola Mae Withnell and their five children. (There would soon be seven; Enola Mae was pregnant with twins.) Over Labor Day weekend, 1961, Richard McLish and David Withnell (himself the proud owner of a white, 1957 Chevy), drove north to Washington state to look for work. Sometime that weekend Enola would realize that a quilt had disappeared, the one she and a daughter were making for another girl on the farm who was leaving to get married. For some reason, the men had taken it with them.

In 1965, Richard Raymond McLish, once again an inmate in the Oklahoma State Penitentiary in McAlester, Oklahoma, must have read an update on the search for Ann Marie Burr. Bev had written the Tacoma News Tribune, which printed her letter reminding people of the fourth anniversary of Ann's disappearance and that the five thousand dollar reward was still being offered. The Associated Press picked up the story, and among the hundreds of newspapers that printed it was one in Oklahoma.

Within days, McLish wrote Don Burr, who shared the letter with the Tacoma police. In the letter, McLish said that he knew Ann's whereabouts. All he asked in exchange for the information was that the reward money be given to his wife and children. He claimed to have been in a car with a man and woman who had abducted Ann. McLish said that the girl was living with the couple in Oklahoma, and he had seen her over the years. He also said that the couple told him they had "gotten the wrong child."

Detective Tony Zatkovich immediately contacted the penitentiary. Buried deep in the Tacoma police report, by now 600 pages long, was a report of a car with two men and a crying girl speeding away from the Burr neighborhood the morning Ann had disappeared. The car had either an Oregon or a California license plate.

As prison officials tried to sort out McLish's story, the head of the Oklahoma State Bureau of Investigation wrote to Charles Zittel, then chief of Tacoma's police department: "It is our feeling that if there is any substance to McLish's statements, the child is in no immediate danger. Moreover, if his association with her abductors is as alleged, precipitant activity at this time would be ill advised. I trust you will agree that a methodical, systematic evaluation of McLish's information and motives is the most appropriate course of action at this time. You will be kept informed of any new developments as they occur. Please be assured of our complete cooperation in this and any other matters of mutual interest." The letter, dated November 22, 1965, was signed by Earl E. Goerke, Director, Oklahoma State Bureau of Investigation.

After two more years of correspondence, both the Tacoma police and Oklahoma corrections officials thought enough of McLish's story to fly him—with guards, in a state-owned airplane—out to Oregon. By then, McLish's story had changed; he and David Withnell had taken Ann Marie Burr. McLish claimed to be so troubled by Withnell's abuse of the little girl they had abducted that he wouldn't give details about what happened. But he did say they had driven from Tacoma back to the bean farm and that Withnell paid McLish to wrap her body in the quilt and bury her three feet deep. They chose a spot close to a tree so that the land wouldn't be plowed and the body found.

On October 11, 1967, an unusually mild, rainy day with temperatures in the sixties, Lt. Maurice Buchholz and Det. Sgt. Fred Mulholland Jr. of the Tacoma Police Department; two Oregon state police officers; members of the Marion County Sheriff's Office, in Salem, Oregon; Marion County District Attorney Gary Gortmaker; and a representative of the Oregon State Crime Lab, met up at Vern Chamberlin's bean farm in Stayton, Oregon.

McLish had sketched a map of the farm. The Chamberlin farm house was on the northern edge of the land; the main road cut west to east across the bean fields. There were footbridges, three shacks, and a pond to the south. McLish had changed his story again; now he said that they had put Ann, wrapped in the blanket, in the pond, not buried by a tree.

Complicating the effort to find her body—if it was on the farm—was the fact that a flood in 1964 had changed the landscape of the land. Vern Chamberlin pointed out that if a small body had been in the pond, it likely would have been washed away in the torrent of water. Chamberlin showed the police how the flood had even moved the path of the road and other identifying landmarks on the farm.

As state police skin divers search the pond in vain, the two Tacoma officers, Lt. Buchholz and Det. Sgt. Mulholland, ducked into one of the shacks to get out of the rain. McLish pointed out that it was the same shack his family had lived in during the summer of 1961.

What little credibility McLish had disappeared when he was caught in a lie. McLish had seemed visibly disturbed by the news they shared with him, that his good friend David Withnell had killed himself December 27, 1963, by carbon monoxide poisoning while sitting in his '57 Chevy. Problem was, McLish already knew. Police concluded that the tears McLish showed on hearing of his friend's death was "a put up deal."

The Tacoma police officers went to see Dave Withnell's widow. Enola Mae had remarried and was living in another small town nearby. She told them the story of the quilt disappearing and the Labor Day weekend the two men had spent in Washington state. She said that she and her seven children had left David Withnell when she learned he had molested one of their daughters. She said her former husband was indeed capable of killing a child; she didn't think Richard McLish was.

While McLish stalled his inevitable return to the Oklahoma prison, police showed his photo to both Donald Burrs, the father of Ann Marie, and the architect. Neither recognized him. That seemed to puzzle McLish who implied he knew Don Burr (Ann Marie's father) and asked repeatedly, "Are you sure Don Burr says he don't know me? "

While he was still in Oregon, McLish agreed to a Sodium Pentothal (or "truth serum") exam, after first consenting to a polygraph, then changing his mind. There is no evidence that he underwent either test.

The guards took McLish back to Oklahoma where he continued his periodic stays in the McAlester prison, finally receiving a long sentence after being convicted of a third felony, another stolen car. His crimes and his stays in prison began to wind down in the 1980s.

Lt. Buchholtz summed up their two-year investigation of McLish and his connection to the disappearance of Ann Marie Burr: "We can't prove he did it, and we can't eliminate him," he told a newspaper.

About the time the Tacoma Police Department was finished with Ralph Everett Larkee and Richard Raymond McLish, its two most memorable crime fighters left, for good this time. Ted Strand retired in March, 1966, and Tony Zatkovich didn't last much longer without him. Zatkovich tried a few other jobs; he served on the Tacoma City Council until he was ousted in a recall effort led by the man who had presided over the wedding of his son, Dick. He ran for Pierce County Sheriff in 1970 but lost. When the Tacoma News Tribune published a story in 1979 looking back at their careers and asking their opinion on how police work had changed, Zatkovich grumbled again that it still was no place for women.

Hadn't Bev and Don had enough heartache? Not long after Ann disappeared, Raleigh Burr witnessed an outburst by Mary. "Bev told Mary to do something and Mary—very shrill—screamed," he explained. "Her response was way too strong." It was one of the first indications that something was very wrong with Mary. Did it date back to the night her sister disappeared?

As Mary plummeted into mental illness, Bev jeopardized her own life and the happiness of her other children to try and save Mary. "I've already lost one daughter," Bev would explain. "I'm not going to lose another."

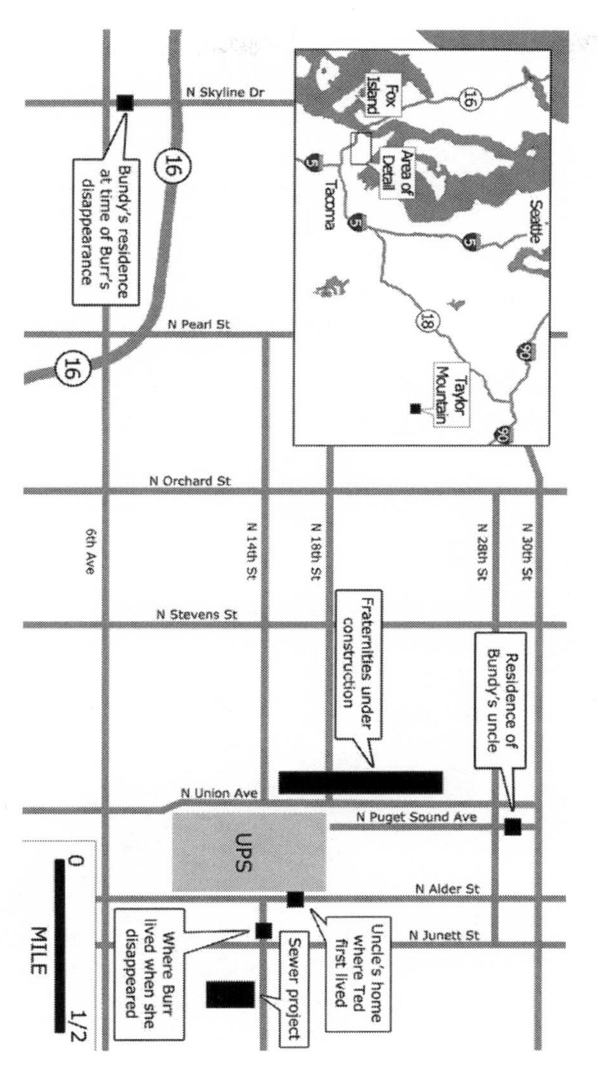

A map of Tacoma showing the proximity of the Burr and Bundy homes, nearby construction projects, and Taylor Mountain, where the skeletons of several victims were found. Map by Brad Arnesen.

Ted Bundy, right, and Doug Holt, center.

Ted Bundy, Sandi Holt, and Doug Holt on Doug's birthday, 1955 or 1956.

Ted's high school yearbook photo, 1965.

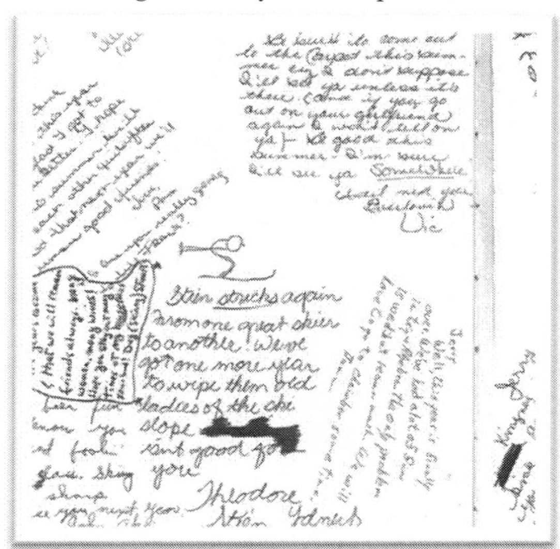

A sketch by Ted in his friend Jerry Bullat's high school yearbook.

Author Ann Rule, who first met Ted when they were volunteers at a Seattle crisis hotline. She was working on a book about the hunt for a serial killer known only as "Ted."

The contents of Ted's VW, with burglary tools, after he was stopped in Utah in 1975 for attempting to evade police. Salt Lake County Sheriff's Department.

Ted waving at a press conference in Tallahassee, Florida after hearing the reading of murder charges against him. Bettmann/Corbis.

Ted makes the FBI's Ten Most Wanted list in 1978.

In court with his lawyers at the first Florida trial, June, 1979. Bettmann/Corbis.

An exhausted Ted, the day after receiving the death penalty for the murder of 12-year-old Kimberly Diane Leach. One of his psychiatrists says there are clues to Ted's mental state in his eyes.

#6094

October 9, 1984

Mr. Ted Bundy
Florida Correctional Facility
Starke, Florida

Dear Mr. Bundy,

I wish to identify myself to you as a Tacoma Psychiatrist, practicing here since 1971. Prior to that I was in State Government appointed to the directorship of the Department of Institutions by Governor Dan Evans.

Among my clientelle is Mrs. Donald (Beverly) Burr. Her daughter, Anne Marie Burr, disappeared from her home on the evening of August 31, 1961. The child was never seen or heard of again.

The effect of this loss to the Burrs is beyond comprehension. You will note that Mrs. Burr is still in treatment dealing with depression, profound anxiety and a series of very difficult acting out behaviors.

It would be very helpful if the Burrs knew the truth about their daughter, ie, what happened to her. If you have any information concerning this child I wish you would advise me.

In the event that you would want to talk to me in private and maintain absolute confidentiality, I would arrange to come to Florida to see you or we could possibly talk by phone.

Sincerely,

William R. Conte, M.D.

WRC:al

Beverly Burr's psychiatrist first wrote to Ted Bundy, Oct. 9, 1984.

Copy of one of our letters to Ted Bundy.

Mrs. Beverly Burr
[illegible]
Tacoma, WA [illegible]

May 30, 1986

Dear Ted,

On August 31, 1961, just before school was to start for you and our children, there came a black rainy night with lots of heavy winds. You were [illegible] and had been wandering the streets late at night and peeping in windows and taking cars. I feel your FIRST MURDER WAS OUR ANN MARIE BURR. The bench from the back yard was used to climb into the living room; the orchard next door was a dark setting for murder. What did you do with the tiny body? God can forgive you.

With all appeals likely to be refused and soon, there is nothing left for you in this world; there can STILL be everything good for you in the next.

Your life started going wrong somewhere when you were very young. There had to be a lot of bad things happen to make you have your strong feelings of hatred.

I came close to ruining my life because of my cruel actions and feeling no sorrow about them. A lot of strange circumstances brought help to me. I would not have found myself, even though I knew I needed help and my actions were getting out of control. You should have received that same help when you needed it.

God can still give the help to you if you can gather together any strength you have left and try to feel a real sorrow inside for the horrors you have brought to so many. You will face these horrors alone if there is no chance to be with God after you die.

You have NOTHING MORE TO LOSE IN THIS WORLD. By explaining your sickness, you will feel sorrow and gain everything in the next life, as God promised you and all of us. Please try. There isn't much time. I am deeply sorry you did not get help when you first needed it. I have not written until now because the end of life for you did not seem near until now. Will you write to me regarding Ann Marie?

Beverly Burr
Mother of Ann Marie Burr

Bev Burr's first letter to Ted Bundy, May 30, 1986.

Beverly Burr
2905 North 28th
Tacoma, Washington

June 8, 1986

Dear Beverly,

Thank you for your letter of May 30.

I can certainly understand you doing everything you can to find your daughter. Unfortunately, you have been misled by what can only be called rumors about me. The best thing I can do for you is to correct these rumors, these falsehoods.

First and foremost, I do not know what happened to your daughter Ann Marie. I had nothing to do with her disappearance.

You said she disappeared August 31, 1961. At the time I was a normal 14-year-old boy. I did not wander the streets late at night. I did not

Ted Bundy's response to Bev, June 8, 1986.

-2-

it from here.

Love yourself.

Peace,

ted

How Ted Bundy usually signed his letters: "peace, ted."

The last victim. Kimberely Leach disappeared from Lake City, Florida, on February 9, 1978. She was twelve years old. *AP/Wide World Photos*

Some of Ted's victims. Top row, left to right: Lynda Healy, Donna Manson, Susan Rancourt, Roberta Kathleen Parks, Brenda Ball, Georgeann Hawkins. World Wide Photos.

Other victims. Top row, left to right: Denise Naslund, Janice Ott, Caryn Campbell, Laura Aime, Debra Kent, Melissa Smith, Lisa Levy, Margaret Bowman. World Wide Photos.

Johnnie and Louise Bundy and Carole Ann Boone, in a Florida courtroom in 1979 as Ted is found guilty of the Chi Omega killings. World Wide Photos.

Local

Expert says Bundy killed girl, 8, when he was 1

Vandals hit high schools on Peninsula after kegger

Solidarity of conscience

1987 newspaper coverage of Ted's hypothetical confession that he killed Ann.

Standing alone in her dining room in Tacoma, Louise Bundy, mother of convicted murderer Ted Bundy, wipes away a tear as she tells her son, 'You will always be my precious son.' He was executed minutes later. (Russ Carmack / Tacoma News Tribune). The photograph was taken the evening of January 23, 1989.

Bev, on a trip, looking unusually content.

Bev and Don Burr with two of their grandchildren, 1993.

Beverly Burr, 46 years after the disappearance of her daughter. (Ellen M. Banner / The Seattle Times). Published October 21, 2007.

My Teacher Says Its Like College

Dear Mom and dad
I hope you can come Sunday
you have to sign in
they look through your bags
the place hasn't changed much
they keep me fairly busy
food is good
got cigarrets and ten dollars today
I bought a plant we have a deck
I want my own apt. when I get out
I started self acertive class
my teacher says it's like college
we have essays and homework
I've been reading my day to day book
tomorrow is clean up campus day
no classes
I got my medication but I need more
I still can't sleep
write back
love
Mary

My Daughter, Thirty-Three Years Old

You go for a walk.
I can't finish the baking.
Will you return? When? How?
You come back in a few hours,
Sad smile, vacant eyes,

Hand me a white shell.
I tell you it's nice.
Part of it is broken,
Like you and my heart.

Mental Illness

Clothes too small,
different from those.
we stored last time you were
evicted,
especially the red dress
with gold spangles.
You smile slyly, what scene
did you imagine.
when you discovered
the soft chiffon.
in a thrift store?
Clerks counted coins
into your hand,
shrugged shoulders,
"a weirdo here!"
We fold jeans, blouses,
try to overlook.
brown-edged eyelets
from cigarette burns.
Like vile garbage vapors,
tobacco fumes saturate.
You'll get a job,
find new friends.
No hospitals, you say. Daughter,
hospitals don't want you.
No one wants you.

We can only give love,
keep sad storage.

Night of Hate I

The night is black.
Rolls of thunder muddle air.
Rain beats against the panes,
Stronger squalls smash bush and flower.
Forceful gusts tear through trees
Breaking limbs, uprooting others.
Soon, rampaging winds must weary.
And hatred leave an evil sky.
I'm alone now, afraid.

Night of Hate II

The night is black, winds blow strong,
Air is filled with thunder's groaning.
Rain beats out unbroken song.
Joined by sounds of distant moaning.
Forceful squalls strike furiously.
And smash each bush and flower.
Savage winds tear through each tree
Breaking limbs with monstrous power.
Night of frenzy, dismal, dreary,
Gusts rage on with ghastly cry.
When will wretched winds grow weary?
When will hatred leave the sky?

Her Son, Her Son

Up the stairs to get
it wasn't a sweater
back down

dishes need washing
no, they're put away
she strains like a caged fox
sinks heavily, rests.
tries not to cry.
how could he possibly be arrested
an ice heart freezes
beneath her flesh

A Pin For Barbie

The moon is such a pretty ball.
And if it weren't so high,
I'd like to pull it from the sky
And bounce it down the hall.
But I would like the best of all
To reach my arm up far
And catch a shiny falling star
To pin on Barbie Doll.

11

Life On Death Row

TED LIKED TO APPEAR BUSY, AND HE WAS NEVER busier than he was on death row. For the nine years and six months that he was incarcerated at the Florida State Prison in Starke, Florida (also referred to by its mailing address, Raiford), he was busy corresponding with dozens of people; he was busy marrying and becoming a father; he was busy "consulting" with police about other serial killers; he was busy telling the prison he was now a Hindu (the only way he could get the prison to feed him a vegetarian cuisine); he was busy cooperating with authors as the subject of their books; he was busy writing his memoirs; he was busy planning to escape (that time it didn't happen); he was busy socializing with his neighbors on death row, including Ottis Elwood Toole, the killer of six-year-old Adam Walsh; and he was busy—until it was too late—shrugging off the possibility that he would be executed. He was even busy thinking how he might serve out his prison time in his home state of Washington.

There will always be questions about exactly when Ted Bundy began killing girls and young women, and about how many murders he committed. We do know when the killings finally ended.

Since childhood, Ted could not stay away from college campuses. It began when he lived at his great-uncle's house near the University of Puget Sound in Tacoma, the campus where he, or someone, most likely disposed of Ann Marie Burr's body. Then, living near the University of Washington in Seattle, his victims included young women he abducted from colleges in several western states. His killings continued as he attended law school in Utah. When he was near a campus he could be inconspicuous, pretend to be the successful, handsome young man others saw, aspire to the life he wanted, and of course, find women who fit his ideal image: young, pretty, with long hair parted in the middle, women of a "certain class," as he described them.

When Ted escaped from a Colorado jail on New Year's Eve, 1977 (his second escape from a jail in six months), his days of facing charges for burglary, aggravated kidnapping, and evading police were over. He had finally been charged with murder, for the death of 24-year-old Caryn Campbell at a Colorado inn where she was skiing with her fiancé and his children. With several hours head start on the police, Ted first went to Chicago, but soon headed to a warmer climate, Florida, and to one of its college towns, Tallahassee. The U.S. Supreme Court had struck down the death penalty, but did Ted know that Florida was the first state to reintroduce it? Some who knew Ted believe he chose Florida for more than the climate; maybe he was ready to be caught. He had to have known the state's reputation for executions. After all, Florida's nickname was "The Buckle of the Death Belt."

Ted moved into a rooming house near the Florida State University. He sat in on classes and ate at the school's cafeteria. All the while he was drinking heavily and stealing wallets, credit cards, keys, cars, license plates, and IDs. In the early morning hours of January 15, 1978, he left a bar and entered the Chi Omega sorority house on the Florida State campus. With a club, he killed two young women, Lisa Levy and Margaret Bowman, and wounded two others, Karen Chandler and Kathy Kleiner; then he walked down the street, entered an apartment, and attacked Cheryl Thomas, also a student. She survived. Three weeks later, he bought a knife and abducted 12-year-old Kimberly Diane Leach from outside her junior high school in Lake City, Florida. Her body wouldn't be found for two months, but five days after Ted killed her, he was stopped by a patrol car in Pensacola. Ted was driving a stolen VW, and after a brief skirmish, he was handcuffed and jailed. The police had no idea they had just arrested one of the FBI's Ten Most Wanted criminals. They wondered why the man, who seemed "strangely depressed," kept repeating, "I wish you had killed me... I wish you had killed me." Bev Burr couldn't believe the coincidence, that the name of his last victim was Leach, Bev's surname.

He was tried first for the Chi Omega killings. Florida jurors never heard of the women he was suspected of killing in five western states. In fact, Ted was never prosecuted for those crimes; Florida was not going to let go of him, and Ted was good at not leaving physical evidence at the scene of his crimes. Ted, who had completed only a couple of semesters of law school (in fact, he had repeated the first year of law school), rejected a plea deal and acted as his own lead attorney. He was found guilty of the Chi Omega killings on July 25, 1979. Louise and Johnnie Bundy, and Ted's friend Carole Boone, were in the courtroom. A reporter wrote that Louise sobbed after hearing the verdict. Another one reported that Ted waved and smiled and that he told a friend he was "perplexed" by the verdict.

Six days later, Ted's mother took the stand during the penalty phase hearing to speak on her son's behalf. Louise told the courtroom, "We tried to be very conscientious parents, ones who did things with our children, gave them the best we could on a middle-class income. But, mostly we wanted to give them lots of love." She told the court that she considered the death penalty "...the most primitive, barbaric thing that one human can impose on another. My Christian upbringing tells me that to take another's life under any circumstances is wrong. I don't believe the State of Florida is above the laws of God."

Those in the courtroom said it was the only time during the long trial that Ted Bundy cried. The same jury that had found him guilty of first degree murder in the Chi Omega killings debated his punishment for one hour and forty minutes. On July 31, 1979,

Louise and Johnnie Bundy heard their son sentenced to death. Louise gasped and closed her eyes in agony. Johnnie held her hand.

The next year Ted was convicted of the murder of Kimberly Diane Leach and again received the death penalty. Neil Chethik covered the trial for the *Tallahassee Democrat.* Ted was more low-key than he had been during the Chi Omega trial. Still, there was a lot of posturing on his part. He enjoyed being watched and whispering to his attorneys. "He was the star of the show," according to Chethik. Louise and Johnnie Bundy did not regularly attend the trial, but once again Louise spoke during the penalty phase. "She said something like, 'My son became very troubled, something happened to him, you shouldn't kill him,'" Chethik remembered.

The dozens of journalists took turns being a designated pool reporter for sessions in the judge's chambers. One day, Chethik was the only reporter in the room with Ted, the judge, and two attorneys. Ted locked eyes with the reporter. Chethik was on the receiving end of the famous Ted stare—the strange stare women mentioned who were lucky enough to walk away from him, the stare that terrified his relatives and even some police. Ted wouldn't look away, so Chethik did, finally.

Like a few other reporters over the years, Chethik had questions about the trials and the evidence against Ted, which was mostly clothing fibers connecting Ted to the Leach murder. "My overall feeling as an observer is that he was guilty," Chethik said. "The [crime] was bloody, messy, disgusting.

But as a juror, I don't believe there was enough to actually convict him beyond a reasonable doubt." But the Leach trial was important to the State of Florida. If Ted ever won an appeal in the Chi Omega killings, the state needed the Leach guilty verdict and death penalty to keep Ted. "The attitude was, 'We need to lock this guy down and kill him,'" Chethik remembered. "The second trial was the knock-out punch." The state wanted to make sure he died in Florida.

The only time Ted spoke during the second trial was at his sentencing. He invoked an old Florida law still on the books allowing him to make a declaration in court and marry his former co-worker, Carole Ann Boone. The two had worked together at Seattle's Department of Emergency Services, a job that enabled him to continue the study of his favorite subject, crime and police procedures; he even reportedly wrote a pamphlet for the agency on rape prevention. Boone was in touch with Ted after he was arrested in Utah, and she and a group of Ted's friends raised some money for his defense.

Soon, she and her teenage son moved to Florida to be closer to Ted. She and Ted reportedly consummated their marriage in a corner of a visitor's room, having bribed a guard to look the other way. Boone became pregnant and gave birth to a daughter. They may have considered themselves married, but the State of Florida never did.

Because of so-called Son of Sam laws prohibiting criminals from profiting from their crimes, Ted couldn't sell his story. But he was looking for a way to find money for Boone and her children. By 1980, there were already four books published about him (including his friend Dick Larsen's *The Deliberate Stranger,* his other friend Ann Rule's *The Stranger Beside Me,* and former girlfriend Liz Kendall's *The Phantom Prince*).

He decided to give unusual access to two journalists; it would be the first time Ted sat for extensive interviews. Reporter Stephen Michaud received a phone call from his agent saying Ted Bundy wanted to cooperate on a book. At that time, Ted was suspected in as many as 150 murders. Michaud teamed up with Hugh Aynesworth, who he knew from when they both worked at *Newsweek.* Ted Bundy may have thought he was the biggest story in America, but Aynesworth had seen much bigger. As a reporter for the *Dallas Morning News,* Aynesworth had witnessed three of the most important events in American history: he saw President John F. Kennedy shot as his motorcade wound through the city; he was present when police arrested Lee Harvey Oswald in a movie theater later the same day; and he saw Jack Ruby shoot Oswald. He was also the first reporter to interview Oswald's widow, Marina Oswald.

Ted said he wanted an impartial, re-investigation of the crimes he had been convicted of and others he was a suspect in. Michaud would interview Ted on death row, while Aynesworth would review all of the evidence against Ted, traveling to the western states where authorities believed Ted had committed dozens of murders. The agreement—made with

Carole Boone's input—quickly became complicated. (According to Aynesworth, Boone was paid some money, either by the publisher of Michaud and Aynesworth's book, *The Only Living Witness*, or a foundation created to help family members of death row inmates.)

It is widely believed that Ted was expecting Michaud and Aynesworth to find information that would clear him as a suspect in the murders. Other authors who wrote about Ted think Michaud and Aynesworth deceived Ted, that they strung him along, never intending to try and prove his innocence. But when Ted wrote to Michaud and Aynesworth about plans for the book, he advised them "not to search for evidence that he was guiltless as he claimed," because the facts were not there. He also stated that he didn't care what they wrote, just so they got it right and "just so it sells." "We thought, 'If we can prove him innocent, great,'" Aynesworth remembered.

Almost immediately, Michaud and Aynesworth decided Ted was guilty. To get at the truth, they needed to find a way to get Ted to open up. He agreed to talk about the crimes in the third-person; he would speculate about the murders without confessing. (Twenty-six years later, O.J. Simpson would try a similar approach with *If I Did It,* his book about the murders of Nicole Brown Simpson and Ron Goldman.) Michaud said Ted "jumped" at the suggestion. "It wasn't long before we were deep into his macabre world, exploring regions of the criminal psyche I hadn't guessed existed," Michaud wrote.

Michaud had the best rapport with Ted, maybe because he was a Tacoma boy, too. They had an astonishing number of experiences in common. Two years younger than Ted, Stephen Michaud had grown up about five miles from Ted in Tacoma. They knew people in common, and they were both born in Burlington, Vermont, and had moved to Tacoma when young. Michaud never knew his birth father, either, although his parents had been married.

Michaud was sickened by Ted's revelations, but he was more patient than Aynesworth. Aynesworth was more than 15 years older than Michaud and Ted and the father of two teenage girls. "He hated me," Aynesworth said of Ted. Ted talked about how he sometimes returned to the decaying bodies days or weeks later. At least once he shampooed a victim's hair and put makeup on her. "If you've got time, they can be anyone you want them to be," he said.

"I'd ask him how he could return to the mountain, visit the corpses and have sex with them," Aynesworth remembered. "He said, 'You had to be there, Hugh.' I said, 'I'd never be there.' "

Some saw Ted's speaking in the third person as a way of confessing, without actually confessing. Without a doubt it was manipulative. Michaud and Aynesworth got some insights into the mind of a serial killer, but it was also a way for Ted to keep the police—and the families of dozens of missing and murdered women—guessing.

Michaud and Aynesworth met with Ted for more than 100 hours, from January, 1980, through March, 1981, wearing out five tape recorders in the process. Michaud would attend the Kimberly Diane Leach trial by day, then interview Ted at night (sometimes by telephone). From the beginning, Ted told them that he "was a victim of incompetent defense attorneys, poisonous pretrial publicity, and manipulated evidence." Michaud and Aynesworth admit that they, like many others in Ted's life, could not tell when he was being genuine. Their time with him was complicated by the fact that Ted was often stoned, according to Michaud.

They heard the familiar stories: of how ashamed Ted was of the Nash Rambler his parents drove; of how he grew up thinking Louise was really his sister; of how much he resented kids with money; of his bitterness towards Louise. The two authors witnessed some of the physical transformation in Ted that others had seen. When Michaud was at the prison, and Ted was talking about murder, he "would grab the recorder and cradle it... a white mark appeared on his left cheek, like a scratch, then it would fade away... " Michaud wrote.

They concluded that Ted had a "strong streak of narcissism, entitlement," and that it was "entirely possible" that Ted's grandfather was his father (he made them promise they wouldn't contact Samuel Cowell). Aynesworth now says that he "never bought" the theory that Ted's grandfather was his father.

They also came to believe that the key to Ted's crimes was possession. "Murder isn't just a crime of lust or violence," Ted told FBI agent Bill Hagmaier when Ted was on death row. "It becomes possession. They are part of you... You feel the last bit of breath leaving their bodies... You're looking into their eyes... A person in that situation is God! "

During the taped sessions with the two journalists, Ted described—in the third-person—how he evolved from stalking a woman to murder.

> *"And we can say that the, the... on one particular evening, when he had been drinking a great deal... and he was passing a bar, he saw a woman leaving the bar and walk up a fairly dark side street. And for no, uh, we'd say that, something seemed to seize him! I was going to say that something crystallized, but that's another way of looking at it. But the urge to do something to that person seized him—in a way he's never been affected before. And it seized him strongly. And to the point where, uh, without giving a great deal of thought, he searched around for some instrumentality to uh, uh, attack this woman with. He found a piece of two-by-four in a lot somewhere and proceeded to follow and track this girl."*

Later, during the same conversation, Ted explained how the impulse escalated.

> *"On succeeding evenings he began to, uh, scurry around this same neighborhood,*

obsessed with the image he'd seen on the evening before. And on one occasion, on one particular occasion, he saw a woman park her car and walk up to her door and fumble for her keys. He walked up behind her and struck her with a ... a piece of wood he was carrying. And she fell down and began screaming, and he panicked and ran."

Then Ted talked about how, after vowing never to do "something like that again," he had trouble controlling his urges.

"And he did everything he should have done. He stayed away from... he didn't go out at night. And when he was drinking, he stayed around friends. For a period of months, the enormity of what he did stuck with him, and he watched his behavior and reinforced the desire to overcome what he had begun to perceive were some problems that were probably more severe than he would have liked to believe they were."

On April 4, 1980, Ted described for Stephen Michaud the last hours of Lynda Ann Healy, the 22-year-old University of Washington psychology major Ted had classes with. During the recording Ted singled out the attack as "one of the first instances that he'd (the unnamed serial killer he is hypothesizing about) abducted a woman in this fashion."

There were things Ted wouldn't discuss, in the third-person or otherwise. Top of the list were any children he was suspected of killing, or had been convicted of killing, including 12-year-old Kimberly Diane Leach.

Eventually, Aynesworth grew impatient with the third-person "confessing" and encouraged Ted to "get it all out and get it done," and truly admit his crimes. He urged him to make a list of names and dates. Maybe it would lessen his guilt. But as Ted told Michaud and Aynesworth, "...I don't feel guilty for anything. I feel less guilty now than I've ever felt in any time of my life... I guess I'm in the enviable position of not having to deal with guilt. There's no reason for it."

It seemed that Ted would never give up his secrets.

It didn't take long for Michaud and Aynesworth to realize that Ted came from what Michaud called "a really, really buttoned-down family." A close family friend, interviewed for a documentary about Ted, described the family as "secretive." (For example, both Ted and his oldest half-sister, Linda Bussey, said they never discussed with each other or with other members of the family who Ted's birth father was.)

Just before Christmas, 1980, Michaud and Aynesworth traveled to Tacoma to talk with Louise and Johnnie Bundy. The four sat in the Bundy living room. Louise was still adamant that Ted was innocent and his convictions were all a mistake. He had done nothing to prepare his mother for the truth.

The two journalists played one of the taped interviews between Stephen Michaud and Ted, where Ted speculated in the third-person about raping and killing a girl.

TB: "... they were at a place where there was an orchard, or a number of trees or something. As he came up behind her she heard him. She turned around and he brandished a knife and grabbed her by the arm and told her to do what he wanted her to do. You know, to follow him. He pushed her off the sidewalk into this darkened wooded area, and uh, told her to submit and do what he wanted her to do.

But he found himself with this girl who was struggling and screaming. Uh, not screaming, but let's say just basically arguing with him. There were houses in the vicinity and he was concerned that somebody might hear. And so, in an attempt to stop her from talking or arguing, he placed his hand over her mouth. So, not thinking clearly but still intending not to harm her, let's say, he placed his hands around her throat."

SM: "Uh huh."

TB: "Just to throttle her into unconsciousness so that she wouldn't scream anymore. She stopped struggling, and it appeared that she was unconscious. but not, in his opinion, to a point where he had killed her.

Then let's say he removed her clothes and raped her and put his own clothes back on. At about that point, he began to notice that the girl wasn't moving.

It appeared, although he wasn't certain, that he'd done what he had promised himself he wouldn't do. And he had done it, really, almost inadvertently.

Uh, so he took the girl by one of her arms and pulled her to a darkened corner of this little orchard and then, in a fit of panic, fled the scene."

"We're playing the tape for her," Michaud explained about Louise's reaction. "She starts to make little noises, like a mouse. I actually thought an animal might be in the room. Then, she suddenly says, 'How about some coffee and apple pie?' "

Bev and Don Burr read the Michaud/Aynesworth book, *The Only Living Witness,* when it was published in 1983. They wondered if one of Ted's stories, the same one Louise Bundy heard him relate on audio tape, was about *their* little girl, about *their* orchard. Bev wrote Hugh Aynesworth, explaining her daughter's disappearance.

"My husband and I read your book slowly, word for word, practically memorizing your book," Bev wrote. And she listed the similarities between Ted and their missing daughter. The orchard. The noises in the yard she heard late at night. How close they lived to the campus where Ted's great-uncle was a music professor. How Ann took piano lessons across the street from the college's music building. The possibility Ted was a paperboy in their neighborhood. The bench police thought a teenager might have used to look through the living room window. The print of a tennis shoe found on the bench and near the basement. The name of Ted's last victim, Leach. Bev also hypothesized that if Ann was Ted's first victim, maybe the publicity regarding her was so great and lasted such a long time that it had prevented him from committing another murder until he reached his twenties.

Bev and Don offered to travel to Texas to see Aynesworth. They thought maybe he and Michaud knew more about Ted's early crimes. Aynesworth remembered Bev's letter to him, but he received hundreds of letters after the book was published, many from families still looking for answers. In fact, the girl Ted described in the orchard wasn't Ann. Aynesworth traveled to Utah while investigating Ted's crimes. The unnamed girl in the orchard was 17-year-old Melissa Smith, the daughter of Midvale, Utah's police chief and one of Ted's victims.

The Burrs never went to Texas to see Hugh Aynesworth. They did travel to Colorado in 1985 to talk to people at the Pitkin County Courthouse in Aspen, where Ted had jumped from a second story window in June, 1977. Bev and Don had heard a rumor that Ted had said something about Ann to the police there, but their trip was fruitless.

So Bev decided to write to Ted. Their correspondence began with a letter from her doctor. On October 9, 1984, Dr. William R. Conte, Mary's psychiatrist, who had become a friend and confidant of Bev's (as well as very concerned with Bev's emotional state), wrote Ted. He identified himself as a Tacoma psychiatrist treating Mrs. Donald (Beverly) Burr:

"Her daughter, Anne [sic] Marie Burr, disappeared from her home on the evening of August 31, 1961. The child was never seen or heard of again. The effect of this loss to the Burrs is beyond comprehension. You will note that Mrs. Burr is still in treatment dealing with depression, profound anxiety and a series of very difficult acting out behaviors. It would be very helpful if the Burrs knew the truth about their daughter, what happened to her... In the event that you would want to talk to me in private and maintain absolute confidentiality, I would arrange to come to Florida to see you or we could possibly talk by phone."

Ted answered Conte within the week:

"Your concern for her (Bev's) well-being and peace-of mind would seem to go beyond the call of duty and this extraordinary demonstration of your compassion moves me in a way that says I can trust you to understand what I have to say.

I have absolutely no knowledge of what happened to Anne [sic] Marie Burr 23 years ago. I had nothing to do with her disappearance. Nothing. At the time I was for all practical purposes a normal, healthy 15-year-old. Even the thought of harming another human being would have been as ghastly and slim as the thought of jumping off the Narrows Bridge...

I have from time–to-time heard the Burr disappearance mentioned in connection with me. With all due respect, I didn't imagine how anyone could have taken such a report seriously. However, I do realize that no stone must be left unturned, but I thought that stone had been turned and discarded long ago."

Bev may never have told her friends or family that she was being treated by Dr. Conte (at one time, letters to Bev from Dr. Conte were sent to Julie in Seattle so that Don wouldn't know about it). Her family knew she was difficult to be around, that she seemed to be in a constant state of anxiety; they knew she seemed to have lots of accidents. As one family member said, "If life wasn't in crisis mode, she would create it."

Bev finally wrote Ted herself in 1986, when it looked as if Ted's execution was imminent. In her first letter to Ted, dated May 30, 1986, Bev wrote.

"With all appeals likely to be refused and soon, there is nothing left for you in this world; there can STILL be everything good for you in the next.

Your life started going wrong somewhere when you were very young. There had to be a lot of bad things happen to make you have your strong feelings of hatred.

I came close to ruining my life because of my cruel actions and feeling no sorrow about them. A lot of strange circumstances brought help to me I would not have found myself, even though I knew I needed help and my actions were getting out of control. You should have received that same help when you needed it.

God can still give the help to you—if you can gather together any strength you have left and try to feel a real sorry inside for the horrors you have brought to so many. You will face these horrors alone if there is no chance to be with God after you die.

You have NOTHING MORE TO LOSE IN THIS WORLD... Will you write to me regarding Ann Marie?"

Again, Ted, a prompt correspondent, answered right away. In his response, dated June 8, 1986, he wrote:

"Dear Beverly, Thank you for your letter of May 30. I can certainly understand you doing everything you can to find your daughter. Unfortunately, you have been misled by what can only be called rumors about me. The best thing I can do for you is to correct these rumors, these falsehoods.

First and foremost, I do not know what happened to your daughter Ann Marie. I had nothing to do with her disappearance. You said she disappeared August 31, 1961. At the time I was a normal 14-year-old boy. I did not wander the streets late at night. I did not steal cars. I had absolutely no desire to harm anyone. I was just an average kid. For your sake you really must understand this."

Ted pointed out that he had lived at the time on Skyline Drive in the west end of Tacoma near the Narrows Bridge. And he claimed, in his letter to Bev, to *not* have heard of Ann's disappearance in 1961. That is hard to believe; at 14, Ted was already roaming the town on his bicycle. He was also a window peeper, a purveyor of pornography, a thief, a boy who liked to drag girls into the woods, and addicted to crime and detective stories. Ann's disappearance was front page news daily in those newspapers he delivered and she lived in a neighborhood he had once lived in, his great-uncle's neighborhood. His letter to Bev continued.

> *"There is also a rumor that I was your paper boy back in 1961. Again, I'm almost certain that I wasn't because, as I said earlier, I would remember news of the abduction, which I do not. My paper route covered an area just north and east of the Narrows Bridge.*
>
> *Again and finally, I did not abduct your daughter. I had nothing to do with her disappearance. If there is still something you wish to ask me about this please don't hesitate to write again. God bless you and be with you, peace, ted."*

In a flourish that many found ironic, he signed most of his letters, *peace, ted.*

At about the same time that Ted began corresponding with Bev Burr and Dr. Conte, he wrote Bob Keppel, the King County police detective who had been chief investigator of the "Ted" murders in the 1970s. It was Keppel's idea to use a computer (back when computers were the size of a refrigerator) to narrow a list of thousands of "Ted" suspects to 25 names, among them Ted Bundy. He was number seven. Before they could focus on him, he was arrested in Utah.

By 1984, Keppel was the chief criminal investigator for the Washington State Attorney General's office and a member of a task force working on what was known as "The Green River Killings." Someone was killing dozens of women, many of them prostitutes, and leaving their bodies near the Green River, southeast of Seattle, and at other sites. Ted, who had slipped away from Washington state authorities because of a lack of physical evidence, wrote to Bob Keppel to offer himself as a consultant on the Green River murders. The task force thought the Green River killings had stopped in 1984, but Ted wrote Keppel that serial killers don't quit.

Ted's first letter to the task force arrived in October, 1984. Ted explained that he could offer "valuable insights" into the Green River Killer (Ted called him "Riverman"). Keppel wrote back and Ted's next letter was 22 pages long. For the next several years, Ted ruminated on Riverman's frame of mind, motives, victim pool, geographic preferences, and dump sites. "Technically, he wasn't any help in actually naming the Green River Killer and catching him," Keppel said. "But in understanding the Green River Killer, he was a big help." It wasn't until 2001 that "Riverman" was caught. Gary Leon Ridgway eventually pled guilty to murdering 49 women; as part of a plea bargain, he was spared the death penalty and received a sentence of life imprisonment without parole in exchange for disclosing the whereabouts of missing women. He is serving his sentence at the Washington State Penitentiary, where Ted fantasized he might serve out his prison term.

Keppel also saw his communication with Ted as an opening to talk about other cases—including unsolved cases attributed to Ted. Although Keppel had spent 15 years investigating Ted Bundy, they hadn't met before Keppel went to Florida in 1984, to meet the man he called his "personal nemesis." They met again before Ted was executed in 1989. Keppel wanted Ted to give him an alibi for eight murders in the Northwest. Ted couldn't. Keppel also asked him about the murder of Lonnie Trumbull and the attack on Lisa Wick, the two stewardesses bludgeoned in their Queen Anne Hill apartment in Seattle in 1966. "Ted was shaking and confused," about the questions, Keppel wrote in *The Riverman-Ted Bundy and I Hunt for the Green River Killer.* Ted had "worked himself into a box, knowing all along that I didn't believe him," and he "desperately tried to recover, stammering and doing verbal backflips," according to Keppel.

> *"No. No. I have no hesitation about talking about things I have done, no hesitation about telling you about what I haven't done, okay? So if I tell you something—I may not tell you something—I might not tell you something right now or every single detail right now, but if I tell you something, you can rely on it. And when I say, yes I did it, or no, I didn't do something, that's the way it is."*

Keppel didn't believe much that Ted had to say. His last question to Ted was about Ann Marie Burr. Ted gave a long-winded answer about how ludicrous the idea was, how he was "a kid" at the time, how his paper route was in a different part of Tacoma, how they went to different schools. But Keppel remembered what Ted had told him the year before: there "were some murders killers never talked about, because they were committed too close to home, too close to family, and of victims who were very young." Ted had told Hugh Aynesworth that committing a murder at age 15 would be "...a much more mystical, exciting, intense, overwhelming experience... " than when older. Keppel wrote that Ted "steadfastly did not want to talk about [the Burr case], and every denial he made was unconvincing."

Ted's execution was set for March 4, 1986. Just a few weeks before, in February, a fledgling attorney was handed a pro bono case that changed her life. A recent University of Minnesota law school graduate working at a Washington, D.C. law firm, Polly Nelson was paying her dues, like other new lawyers; that week she was assigned to research the rules and regulations for frozen dairy products. She was asked if she would like to take on a pro bono project for her firm. There was a death penalty case in Florida. Did she know who Ted Bundy was? She wasn't sure, but soon she was representing the man who had been called "the nation's most despised killer."

Ted was under two separate death sentences in Florida, one for the Chi Omega killings and the other for the murder of Kimberly Diane Leach. He was awaiting execution for the Chi Omega murders when Nelson was brought in.

She felt the best chance of getting a stay of execution was to show how Ted had sabotaged his defense. Ted had displayed "irrational conduct" in court, including his "obnoxious posturing for the press, his disrespectful and destructive bantering with Judge Cowart, his utter lack of concern for what the jury saw or heard," according to Nelson. In one of his most damaging displays of ego, Ted insisted on participating in the questioning of witnesses. His public defenders had worked hard to keep the grisly details of the Chi Omega killings out of the courtroom. But Ted introduced all the gruesome minutia for the jury to see and hear. The result was "chaos," according to one of his attorneys, and the move alienated both judge and jury. Ted also prevented his lawyers from addressing his mental competence during the penalty phase and turned down a plea bargain.

Nelson described Ted's conduct in court this way: "Egocentricity, even at the cost of his own best interests." Nelson believed there was another error committed, too. The jury in the Chi Omega murders had been hung at six to six for life or death; the judge erroneously instructed them that they were required to break the tie. Without that instruction, Ted would have been given a life sentence.

Reluctantly, because he didn't believe he was incompetent, Ted agreed to Nelson's petition. Work could proceed on the appeals. Just days before he was to be executed, the Florida Supreme Court denied a stay of execution but the U.S. Supreme Court granted one. He was so close to being executed that Ted had been measured for a casket. For the next three years Ted would be just a hair's breadth away from execution.

Nelson was never swayed by the charm that others saw. Ted wanted her to see him as he saw himself, smart, charming, sophisticated. She didn't. "What he always reminded me of was a stereo salesman," she said. "Glib, seemingly competent, until he was off script." Where others had seen intellect, even brilliance, she saw a man "about as intelligent as a fair-to-middling college undergraduate... he could talk and write, but he couldn't comprehend or respond... he was incapable of independent thought or elaboration." Nelson also described him as "...like a precocious ten-year-old... very literal."

At that time, Ted was still claiming he was innocent of all the murders attributed to him. Ted told Nelson, "Believe me, Polly, I am not the kind of person who would hurt a fly... " She didn't believe that, but she had entered the case with what she calls "naïve optimism," hoping for the "miniscule possibility that Ted had been convicted falsely." Nelson and Ted hadn't talked in detail about his crimes; he was afraid she would be revolted. So was she. Her assignment was to dispute his trials, not be involved in the details of the crimes. But with the Chi Omega execution on hold he now faced execution for the murder of Kimberly Leach. Nelson needed to know if there was a chance he had not, in fact, killed her. Nelson really did not want him to be guilty of killing the child.

She finally put it to him. She asked Ted if there was any mistake; could the girl have been killed by someone else? He stared at her and eventually shook his head. It was, Nelson said, his first direct admission of guilt.

Dr. Dorothy Otnow Lewis calls herself "the last woman to kiss Ted Bundy—and live to tell about it." A psychiatrist and a professor at Yale and at New York University School of Medicine, Lewis was researching death row inmates. Nelson asked if Lewis would meet with Ted Bundy. Lewis' work centered on the search for evidence of childhood abuse. That, she believed, was a key to understanding criminal behavior because abuse appeared to change the anatomy of the brain. Specifically, damage to the prefrontal cortex compromises our ability to know the difference between good and bad choices, and to suppress emotional or sexual urges. In 1986, the year she met Ted, Lewis and her frequent collaborator, Dr. Jonathan Pincus, published a study of 14 juveniles condemned to death; all had suffered severe head injuries in childhood and nearly all had been so traumatized they couldn't remember being abused. Lewis and Pincus believed that the most vicious criminals, are, "...overwhelmingly, people with some combination of abusive childhoods, brain injuries, and psychotic symptoms... "

Lewis began talking with Ted, as well as combing his medical records and talking to family members. She was not impressed with Ted's bravado. When he first met her, he boasted, "I've had seven books written about me!" She said, "Well, I'm dyslexic and haven't read any of them! "

After meeting with Ted, Lewis "bypassed the small talk and blurted out her diagnosis" to Nelson. "Did you know that your client is bipolar?!" she asked Nelson. It was the first evidence that Ted had a recognized mental illness that might have impaired his judgment at his trials. Lewis said that Ted had been "severely mentally ill" since his teenage or college years.

Trying to get anecdotal evidence from Ted's family was not easy. Nelson said that Louise Bundy took "an immediate dislike to Dr. Lewis and insisted that Ted was innocent and that there have never been any problems." But Ted's relatives in the east—the aunts who had sent him west, away from his grandfather—did confide in the psychiatrist. Dr. Lewis began to hear the stories about Ted scaring people with knives and about his grandmother's hospitalizations for manic depression. In a rare moment of candor during the three years when execution seemed imminent, Louise Bundy told Dr. Lewis and Polly Nelson, "I can't wait until it's all over."

Lewis' critics claim she is sympathetic to killers and that anyone can claim they were abused as children. She usually testifies for the defense in death penalty appeals, and has done so for some of the most famous death row inmates in the country, including Mark David Chapman (who shot John Lennon), and serial killer Arthur Shawcross (who cut out and ate the vaginas of some of his victims). Lewis hadn't believed in multiple personality disorder until she met Shawcross, who she says has three personalities; she said she has seen multiple personalities in at least a dozen of the 150 to 200 prisoners she has studied.

At Ted's competency hearing Lewis testified that Ted had a lifelong mental illness which she diagnosed as a bipolar mood disorder (also called manic depression). At the same hearing, his co-counsel in both the Chi Omega and Lake City (Leach) trial said Ted had seemed "disinterested" in the trials, fought any suggestion of an insanity defense, and showed no concern about the possibility of receiving the death penalty. But a psychiatrist who examined Ted for the state called him "brilliant," and said Ted knew "the gravity of the charges." The request for a new trial, on the grounds that Ted had not been competent to help in his defense, was denied.

Hugh Aynesworth went to Florida for the competency hearing. It had been several years since he and Stephen Michaud had spent time with Ted and published their book. Ted wouldn't make eye contact with Aynesworth in the courtroom. It was the first he had heard of Ted's abusive grandfather, the knives incident, and Ted's manic depression.

In May, 1986, as Nelson worked on Ted's appeals, NBC was getting ready to air a two-part television movie, *The Deliberate Stranger,* based on *Seattle Post-Intelligencer* reporter Richard Larsen's book about Ted. Ted was portrayed by Mark Harmon, formerly of *St. Elsewhere* and *People* magazine's "Sexiest Man Alive" that year. Harmon told reporters that he found the role so emotionally harrowing, it kept him awake nights. He said even his dogs didn't know him.

Ted didn't watch the movie (he said he was afraid it's portrayal of him would make him angry), but Nelson watched a tape of it the next day. She found it "stunningly accurate."

After the movie aired, Ann Rule received letters and phone calls from teenage girls convinced they were in love with Ted; they wanted to go to Florida and save him. Rule told each of them that they weren't in love with Ted Bundy; they were in love with Mark Harmon.

Besides the hordes of young women who wrote directly to him (therefore not getting Ann Rule's good advice), Ted corresponded with Rule, Beverly Burr, a niece of Bev's, John Hinckley Jr. (who had tried to assassinate President Ronald Reagan in 1981 in order to impress actress Jodie Foster), and many others. Polly Nelson saw it all as more of Ted's "phony" persona. "His letters were extremely patronizing and condescending," she said. She didn't like the way he would presume an intimacy with anyone and everyone. His psychiatrist became "Dorothy," Beverly Burr became "Beverly," her doctor became "Bill."

Dorothy Otnow Lewis wasn't the only clinician or academician studying serial killers who sought to include Ted Bundy in their research. Dr. Ronald Holmes, an associate professor of criminal justice at the University of Louisville's School of Justice Administration, was also corresponding with Ted. In

1986, before Lewis ever met Ted, Holmes had three lengthy interviews with him, totaling about 24 hours. Holmes had a two-year grant to study serial killers in the U.S. His work didn't make news until he talked about Ted Bundy at a seminar in Boulder, Colorado, in 1987, and said Ted had implied he might have committed his first murder and rape when he was young.

"Expert Says Bundy Killed Girl, 8, When He Was 14," read the headline in the *News Tribune* on May 9, 1987. Bev Burr was photographed holding what the caption described as "a few tattered but preserved mementos of her missing child and the failed search to find her." The story said that during interviews the previous year, Ted Bundy told Ron Holmes that he had "stalked, strangled and sexually mauled his first victim, an eight-year-old girl who mysteriously vanished from her Tacoma home 26 years ago," and that he had "stashed the body of Ann Marie Burr in a muddy pit, possibly near the University of Puget Sound." Only when one reads on is it clear that Ted—again—had been speaking hypothetically.

"This is what he told me," Holmes stated. "He said he knew Ann because of someone's paper route; she helped him deliver his papers occasionally. He said he had been in the house before. He entered her house by the side window, walked past the parent's bedroom, and up some steps. He coaxed her out, downstairs. There was an apple orchard next door. He raped her, killed her, dumped her in a ditch in front of the house, maybe a sewer line. The next day he went over and watched the police talk to the

Burr's on the front porch. He kicked dirt around with his foot. He said she had a crush on him. He said it was his first murder but he had thought about it before. I believe what he told me is absolutely true," Holmes explained. "There is no doubt he knew her."

Ted also played the numbers game with Holmes, reportedly telling him that he had committed more than 300 murders in 10 states, not the 20 or 30 murders attributed to him.

As opposed to the earlier interviews with Michaud and Aynesworth, and later sessions with Bob Keppel and Dr. Lewis and Polly Nelson, the prison wouldn't let Holmes take in a tape recorder, so none of Ted's revelations to Holmes are on tape.

Of course, Ted wanted something from Holmes. He asked Holmes to buy Carole Boone a home computer. Holmes told Ted that if he was going to buy a PC for anyone, it would be one of his children in college. "He dropped me then," Holmes said.

A story in the *Seattle Times* about Holmes' revelations quoted retired Tacoma Police department detective Ted Strand as saying he worked on the Burr case for more than five years, "and we never once had Ted Bundy as a suspect; he was just a kid." A Tacoma police department spokesman told the *News Tribune* that they had no evidence linking Bundy to the Burr case and had no plans to reopen their investigation based on Holmes' theory.

However much Holmes was discounted—and he was, by Bill Hagmaier of the FBI, by Ann Rule, by

Bob Keppel, and by others—it gave Bev and Don Burr the first hope they had experienced in years that they would find out what happened to Ann. And it might have been one of the times Ted was telling the truth. By 1999, the Tacoma police department was giving weight to the Burr-Bundy connection.

Sometime in the last few months of his life Ted explained to FBI agent Bill Hagmaier who he considered his "best friends" and "his family." One was Hagmaier, who Ted had come to know. The other members were John and Marcia Tanner, his "spiritual advisers," and a woman named Diana Weiner.

"I got to know Ted pretty well," Hagmaier said. "One of the ways I related to Ted, we were similar in age, education, we both had a young daughter." Hagmaier specialized in criminal personality profiling and later in his career consulted on dozens of high profile cases, including the JonBenet Ramsey case and the hunt for the Green River Killer. As Ted had offered to consult with Bob Keppel, he had also offered himself to the FBI. Hagmaier met with Ted on and off for years—without Polly Nelson's knowledge. She was not pleased when she found out.

Hagmaier said Ted brought up the case of Ann Marie Burr several times. "I can say one of the things he was genuinely concerned about was that after he was gone, people would pile it on," and blame him for murders he had not committed, Hagmaier said.

"He said, 'Look, I didn't do that one, I couldn't have done it.'" Hagmaier said he doesn't believe everything Ted told him, but he never caught him in a lie, either. Hagmaier also said Ted like to "jerk the chain" of others, and he may have been doing that when he confessed to Ronald Holmes.

John Tanner was a Florida attorney; he and his wife Marcia were born-again Christians who visited Ted as part of their lay ministry. At the end of Ted's life, they described him as "a Christian, remorseful for his actions and earnest in his desire to help ease the pain of his victim's families by confessing to his crimes."

The fourth member of what Ted now called "his family" was Diana Weiner, a Sarasota lawyer married to another attorney. In late 1986, Polly Nelson got word that a "scantily clad young woman" was visiting Ted. Dr. Art Norman—who had evaluated Ted before Dr. Lewis joined the team—told Lewis he'd brought in Weiner to "soften Ted up," maybe get Ted to go along with plans for the competency hearing. Both Nelson and Lewis were suspicious of Weiner. She claimed Ted was entitled to another attorney—her—to handle his civil matters since the prison was involved in a lawsuit with its inmates. Lewis and Nelson were worried that Ted was being manipulated and tried to prevent her access to him, but Ted only grew closer to Weiner, especially after Carole Boone left Florida.

"Ted was offered a lot of money and sex to cooperate," Hagmaier said about the numbers of people wanting something from Ted at the end of his life. Another person who wanted something from Ted was the radio evangelist and psychologist James Dobson. Ted had contacted Dobson about an interview, and Ted's estate or Carole Boone probably benefitted financially from it. It was videotaped, and seen or heard via Dobson's radio show, by millions of people. Dobson's work had focused on the dangers of pornography for years. He had been a member of the 1985 Meese Commission on Pornography (commissioned by U.S. Attorney General Edwin Meese).

The interview was taped the day before Ted was executed. Dobson asked him what the "antecedents" of his behavior was. Ted began by saying there was no physical, sexual, or emotional abuse in his childhood and that he grew up in a wonderful home. And then, Ted explained tearfully how he was influenced by pornography, beginning at a young age.

> *Ted: "As a young boy of 12 or 13, I encountered, outside the home, in the local grocery and drug stores, softcore pornography. Young boys explore the sideways and byways of their neighborhoods, and in our neighborhood, people would dump the garbage. From time to time, we would come across books of a harder nature—more graphic. This also included detective magazines, etc., and I want to emphasize this. The most damaging kind of pornography—and I'm talking from hard, real, personal experience—is that that involves violence and sexual violence. The wedding of those two forces—as I know only too well—*

brings about behavior that is too terrible to describe.

Before we go any further, it is important to me that people believe what I'm saying. I'm not blaming pornography. I'm not saying it caused me to go out and do certain things. I take full responsibility for all the things that I've done. That's not the question here.

The issue is how this kind of literature contributed and helped mold and shape the kinds of violent behavior."

JCD: "It fueled your fantasies."

Ted: "In the beginning, it fuels this kind of thought process. Then, at a certain time, it is instrumental in crystallizing it, making it into something that is almost a separate entity inside."

Ted talked about how alcohol further reduced his inhibitions. And then he went on to warn others who, like him, are vulnerable to violence in the media, "particularly sexualized violence."

Ted: "Those of us who have been so influenced by violence in the media, particularly pornographic violence, are not some kind of inherent monsters. We are your sons and husbands. We grew up in regular families. Pornography can reach in and snatch a kid out of any house today. It snatched me out of my home 20 or 30 years ago. As diligent as my parents were, and they were diligent in protecting their children, and as good a Christian home as we had, there is no protection against the kinds of influences that are loose in a society that tolerates [pornography]... "

The interview didn't air until after Ted's death. Stephen Michaud and Hugh Aynesworth called it "pure theater" and believed that Ted was engaged in "image burnishing." In an article in the *New York Times,* publisher and pornographer Al Goldstein called the Dobson interview "Ted's last lie." Ann Rule thought Ted was manipulating Dobson. Even Carole Boone said Ted was telling people what they wanted to hear. But Polly Nelson said Ted was sincere in "wanting to get his message across about the dangers of violent pornography."

Finally, in January, 1989, Ted ran out of time. He was very busy on his last day. He signed his five-page will; it was witnessed by three people and notarized. It provided "...for the payment of debts and expenses, payment of taxes, gifts of personal property, funeral arrangements, forwarding of mail after his death," and appointed Diana Weiner as his personal representative. The will mentioned that Ted hoped to have his ashes scattered in the mountains of his home state.

Ted met with law enforcement authorities from Washington and Colorado but cancelled a meeting with police from Utah. No explanation was given. He gave investigators details on at least nine murders which he had been suspected of but never charged with. The Seattle Post-*Intelligencer* said Ted confessed "to most of the thirty-six murders he had been suspected of in Washington, Utah, and Colorado between 1974 and 1975," and he also took responsibility for two murders in Idaho to which he had not been previously linked. He confessed to a murder in California, but authorities there have not attributed a killing to him. (In 2011 there were new efforts to rule Ted Bundy in or out as a suspect in unsolved cases in several states.)

The newspaper reported that he appeared "shaken and at times sobbing." Bill Hagmaier told the Florida prosecutor's office that night that Ted could be linked to 50 murders. Dr. Art Norman put the number at 100. Ted had told Florida police that the number was three figures. He admitted to killings in six states; the FBI says it was seven. Ted told Ron Holmes he had committed murders in 10 states. Ted never admitted to his last murders, those of the two Chi Omega women and young Kimberly Diane Leach.

Ted also denied killing the two coeds at the New Jersey shore in 1969, and the murder of a young woman who worked at a motel next door to The Elizabeth Lund Home for Unwed Mothers in Burlington, Vermont. Ted had made a trip to Burlington (presumably in 1969) to try and learn more about his birth. The murder in Vermont happened July 19, 1971. It fit his modus operandi—the young woman was bludgeoned and raped—and an FBI report documenting his life between birth and death is nearly blank for that year. He attended the University of Washington and was working at a medical supply company. But his employment record, at whatever job he held, was notoriously spotty, and even Liz Kendall, his girlfriend, said he disappeared for days at a time. It is a tremendous coincidence—the murder of a 24-year-old woman near the place where Ted was born and temporarily abandoned. Ann Rule believed he might have been responsible for the crime.

Stephen Michaud and Hugh Aynesworth had asked to see him before he was executed, but he refused. Ted cancelled a news conference with 30 journalists that he had arranged. For about a week, Ted had been offering to trade more information about his killings in return for a delay in his execution. He even asked the families of his victims to intervene on his behalf; if they asked for a temporary stay of execution, he would have the time to give details about other missing girls. But Gov. Bob Martinez said he would not "negotiate with a killer."

Ted asked to see Dr. Lewis again. She had seen him in the morning, and wasn't permitted a second visit, but Polly Nelson was. Diana Weiner was present. Nelson and Weiner sat on one side of a glass partition; Ted sat on the other. Nelson told him about two last-minute appeals she was waiting to hear on, one in the Florida Supreme Court and the other in the U.S. Supreme Court.

Ted had various requests to sort through and there was one he wanted to talk to Nelson about. He had received a letter, supposedly from a doctor, offering to switch brains with him (presumably for research purposes). A more valid request came from Dr. Lewis. She asked Ted if he would agree to leave his brain for research, and had drafted a waiver for him to sign. Ted was interested in the possibility that he might have some brain defect that would explain his crimes. But Weiner was opposed to any part of Ted being denied a final resting place. In the end, he did not sign the waiver to donate his brain, although rumors got around: Bob Keppel heard that someone had kept Ted's brain.

Ted had told Dr. Lewis earlier in the day that while everyone else wanted to know *what* he did, she was the only one who wanted to know *why.* He told her how he hadn't known anything was wrong until he was "...twelve, fourteen, fifteen... " At one point, he asked her to turn off her tape recorder. She has never shared what their final conversation was, except to say that he discussed "how very, very young" he was when he began thinking about murder; he also wanted to talk about his rage at his mother. His "last thoughts and words were about his deep confusion and anger toward his mother," Lewis said.

As their time came to an end, Lewis had planned to shake his hand and wish him well. But he suddenly kissed her on the cheek. She instinctively reached up and kissed him back. When she got home that night, she told her husband, also a psychiatrist, that she was "the last woman to kiss Ted Bundy." That's when her husband added, "And live to tell about it."

Ted asked Nelson to use his interviews with her and Dr. Lewis "to explain that he was not a monster." And then he stared into her eyes and asked if she and her co-counsel, Jim Coleman, had "liked" him. "Of course, Ted, of course," she told him.

Nelson was called out of the room and got word that the Florida Supreme Court had ruled against Ted. When she returned, Ted had written a note. He wasn't allowed to pass anything to her, so he held it up against the glass. "I hope you liked me. I hope this wasn't just an unpleasant legal chore for you. I feel close to you now," it read. It was a touching moment, but Nelson said that even in Ted's last hours she never saw any remorse. "He felt sorry for himself but there was no sense of responsibility," Nelson said.

The U.S. Supreme Court voted 5-4 against granting Ted a stay of execution. Nelson had left the prison by the time she heard the news, and telephoned Ted to tell him. He was quiet, and they said their goodbyes. Nelson believed both the Florida Supreme Court and the U.S. Supreme Court were afraid to risk the "public outrage" that would follow another stay. Nelson called Louise Bundy and Carole Boone to tell them that time and hope were running out. "They were furious with Ted and felt deeply betrayed that he had publicly confessed without telling them first," Nelson wrote. Ted's last-minute revelations to police were all over the news. Nelson did not want to attend the execution, and asked Jim Coleman to go.

Ironically, Nelson was let go by her law firm three weeks after Ted was executed. Although it had asked her to take the pro bono case, her firm came to believe that *she* was somehow responsible for the long, "unsavory," million dollar case. "It ruined the law for me. I never went back to litigation," she said. She didn't practice law again for 10 years, and then only because she began to specialize in business law. Nelson never disputed Ted's guilt, but later wrote that, "...in seeing to prevent the killing of a person, I felt I was fulfilling a lawyer's highest calling."

Ted's only contact visitors that evening—meaning they could sit with him without the glass separation—were John and Marcia Tanner. Nelson saw them entering as she left the prison in tears. "You two will be the last to see Ted," Nelson said. "No, we won't. The last will be Our Lord, Jesus Christ," they told her, their eyes cast "skyward, their faces beaming."

In the end, Ted had only his "best friends," as he had described them to FBI agent Bill Hagmaier—the Tanners, Diana Weiner, and Hagmaier. Maybe they took the place of others who had given up on him. So many people in his life were not consoling him, not listening endlessly to him, no longer buying his lies.

Carole Ann Boone, her son, and her daughter with Ted were long gone. They had moved back to the Seattle area in 1986. The original move back was said to be because Carole's mother had been injured in a car accident. An acquaintance of Carole's believed that the notoriety of the case made it impossible for her to stay in Florida, and she was hurt by Ted's relationship with Diana Weiner. According to Ted's sister, his cousin, his attorneys, the police and the journalists who befriended Carole, no one knows where she and her daughter are. Ted's cousin, Edna Cowell Martin, says the family never discusses her. Hugh Aynesworth believed that it was Carole Boone's choice to keep herself and her children away from Ted's family all these years.

Ted's mother and step-father, and his half-siblings, did not go to Florida to say goodbye, something Polly Nelson found sad. In fact, his mother had not seen him for nearly two years before he was executed. Ted's oldest sister, Linda Bussey, is angered when asked why no one went to see Ted. There was "no need" for an in-person goodbye, she said. Bussey dismisses the confessions Ted made the last week of his life, as he confirmed and shared information with various law enforcement agencies. She believed Ted did it because he was "bored."

Regardless, his family has something sadly in common with the parents, family members, and friends of the girls and women he killed. "Have you had anyone close to you murdered? Have you? It's a horrible thing," Bussey said over and over, her voice filled with hurt and anger. To his family, Ted was a victim and was murdered, too. She's correct about that; he was murdered. His death certificate from the State of Florida lists "homicide" as the cause of his death.

In a story in the Tacoma News Tribune a few days before the execution, reporter Chuck Doud wrote about Don Burr's reaction to the impending death of Ted Bundy: "We've lived all our lives with Ted Bundy," Don said. "I will personally be relieved that, come Tuesday, this will all be over." Don had never forgotten the face of the teenager he had seen standing near a ditch at the UPS campus and watching the search for Ann. With time, it had become Ted's face. In a scene that sounds more like something out of the 1950s than 1989, Bev and Don spent the eve of Ted's execution listening to the radio, hoping to hear that he had confessed to more killings, specifically Ann's, prior to his death. He did not.

That evening, January 23, 1989, Doud and photographer Russ Carmack, of the Tacoma News Tribune, waited with Louise and Johnnie Bundy in their home in North Tacoma. A minister was present, but they were the only reporter and photographer. Carole Boone had introduced Doud to the Bundy's a few years before. "I began to know the family then," Doud recalled. "For some reason, they came to think, 'When Chuck calls, he'll at least treat us fairly.'" They may have trusted him because he held different views than most other reporters. Doud was skeptical of some of the evidence against Ted, including the bite marks made on Lisa Levy's buttocks and nipple during the Chi Omega sorority killings (still a controversial subject). "I don't think any of those cases would stand up today," Doud says. And Doud was critical of his peers. He was an editor at the paper and supervised other writers. But after Ted Bundy was arrested in Utah, he was concerned that there had been "no fair coverage" of the case. "From the beginning, the press began to make the case against Ted Bundy," Doud said. He went to Aspen, Colorado to cover Ted's first jail escape; when Ted was captured six days later the press was "jumping for joy, and saying, 'We finally got him,'" Doud explained.

In fact, Doud played a part in Ted's nearly-successful plea deal. Carole Boone had brought some of Ted's attorneys to Tacoma to meet with his family so they could encourage him to plead guilty to second-degree murder in the two Chi Omega cases and for the murder of Kimberly Leach. If he had, he would have avoided execution. "The plea was worked out in my living room," Doud recalled. But Ted turned it down. According to Ann Rule, there were rumors about Ted's "almost" guilty plea, but it was never reported in the press.

Doud still has questions about the extent of Ted's crimes. "Ted Bundy was a thief, a liar, a small-time crook, but did he kill all those people? I have huge doubts," Doud said. "He was a crook, not a saint. He may have killed someone."

A few minutes before 11 p.m. on January 23, 1989, the call came that his parents had been waiting for. When the telephone rang, Louise moved into to the dining room and Russ Carmack followed her. He had his Leica with him, an exceptionally quiet camera. He leaned against a wall and listened to her conversation with Ted. "She kept looking down," Carmack said. He took only a few photos, not wanting to intrude on the scene. He remembers the house was "dark and moody, like the event." Johnnie, his eyes red, spoke briefly to Ted and paced the floor, calling Ted "son."

"We just want you to know how much we love you and always will," his mother told Ted. Doud wrote that Louise's voice "quivered with emotion" as she spoke with him. Prison authorities had allowed 10 minutes for the call. As she listened to Ted, his mother was writing down messages from him for friends and family. At one point, Louise said into the phone, "Chuck Doud is here. Do you want to talk to him?" and she handed the phone to Doud. "[Ted] said, 'Well, I guess I made a few mistakes,'" Doud remembered. Doud told Ted, "Your mom is a tower of strength." Then Doud told Ted his prayers were with him, and handed the phone back to Louise.

In the iconic photograph, Louise is holding the telephone in her left hand and in her right hand is a white pencil. "People always thought it was a cigarette, but it wasn't," Carmack said. "It was exhausting, my heart was racing. I fired off three frames. She finally said goodbye." It was Carmack who heard her say her final words to Ted; he shared them with Doud: "You'll always be my precious son."

"He sounds wonderful," Louise said to the others when the call ended. "He sounds very much at peace with himself. He said, 'I'm sorry I've given you all such grief... but a part of me was hidden.' "

Then the phone rang again. One of Ted's sisters had refused to take his phone call, so he was permitted to call his mother again. The photo of Louise Bundy in the foreground, alone at her dining room table speaking to her son, was taken during the first call. "She was wiping tears from her eyes. She whispered goodbye," Carmack remembered.

Carmack had a long career as a photo journalist. The assignment that night was the hardest. The father of four, Carmack said he offered his condolences as he left the house. Carmack's photo was sent around the world by the Associated Press, but first he had to get it back to the *News Tribune* offices. "They literally stopped the presses to wait for my photo," he said.

Ted was offered a traditional last meal of steak, eggs, hash browns, orange juice, and coffee after turning down an offer to choose his last meal. His head was shaved. He changed into clean prison-issued shirt and pants.

Theodore Robert Bundy, age 42, was executed by electrocution on January 24, 1989 for the murder of 12-year-old Kimberly Diane Leach.

Time of death was 7:16 a.m. It took about 60 seconds for him to die. The scene outside the prison was described as a "carnival atmosphere." Hundreds of people held signs reading "Fry, Bundy, Fry, Thank God It's Fry-Day," and clapped, cheered, sang, and set off fireworks when prison officials announced his death. Within an hour, the body was transported 23 miles to a funeral home in Gainesville.

At 8:38 a.m., the postmortem began.

12

Bev and Don and Louise and Johnnie

WITHIN DAYS OF HIS DEATH, PHOTOS OF A DEAD Ted—authenticated by the medical examiner—were published in the supermarket tabloid *Weekly World News.* "We've been selling them like crazy today," a sales clerk at Dawn's News & Smoke Shop, in Lake Worth, Florida said of the brisk sales.

A director at the Williams-Thomas Funeral Home in Gainesville, where Ted's body had been taken, turned down thousands of dollars in bribes from photographers. *Someone* took a picture or leaked the coroner's photo. There Ted is, his head shaved, with burn marks on his skull from the electrode that had sent two thousand volts of electricity to his brain. An incision runs around the top of his head, from ear to ear, the cut the medical examiner made during the autopsy.

While people in the east were buying up the published photo, sentiment in the west was running against allowing Ted's ashes to be scattered in the Cascade Mountains. Callers to a Seattle radio show suggested other places the ashes could be disposed of, including a sewer or down a toilet. Authorities said there was no federal or state law preventing the dispersing of a serial killer's ashes anywhere he wanted.

Two weeks after Ted's execution, Louise Bundy gave her most extensive interview ever, to *Vanity Fair* writer Myra MacPherson. Standing in the dining room where Russ Carmack photographed her saying goodbye to her son, Louise pointed out the 400 condolence cards piled on the dining room table. Some were simply addressed to: Louise Bundy, Ted's Mother, Tacoma, Washington. *Vanity Fair* photographed Louise embracing Ted's Scout uniform.

Referring to Ted's crimes as "those terrible things," Louise broke her silence about her parents and talked about the environment Ted spent his first years in, revealing that her father had beaten her mother "once in a while." She also admitted to ambivalent feelings about keeping Ted and not putting him up for adoption. And then Louise served MacPherson apple pie.

Life was never normal for Bev and Don, or Louise and Johnnie, but it did return to a routine after Ted was executed. Johnnie continued to work as a cook at the military hospital near Tacoma, and Louise spent years working on the University of Puget Sound campus, where she was well-liked and staff and faculty were fiercely protective of her. They had always lived modestly, and it couldn't have been easy for them to bail Ted out of jail more than once, or to travel and be present when he stood trial.

Don relented and Bev finally got out of the house and had the chance to take writing classes. She worked as a secretary at Bates Technical College and St. Joseph's Hospital, and as a volunteer she taught reading at a local school. Don continued his job at the National Guard base.

Whether planned or coincidental, Bev and Don would often be out of the country in August. They traveled to China, Russia, Iceland, Germany, Canada, Arizona, Cape Cod, the Panama Canal, California, Patagonia, Bermuda, Nova Scotia, and across Asia. They even ran into the Bundy's. Their paths didn't cross often in Tacoma, but they did on a 20-day bus tour of the Ozarks. "There we were, alphabetically, Bundy, Burr," Bev remembered. "Twenty days looking at them!" The two couples didn't speak and seem to have stayed out of each other's photographs.

With the instincts of a journalist, Bev kept a journal of every trip, typing up her notes after she returned home and filling dozens of albums with her observations as well as photographs. If she had a dream about Ann, she recorded it. If she lit a candle for Mary in a church in France, she wrote of it. Both she and Don looked at faces when they traveled, looking for someone who seemed familiar, maybe a little girl grown up. Ann's disappearance was never far from Bev's thoughts. An album of a foreign trip or of a daughter's wedding back home would conclude with newspaper clippings about Ann, updates on Ted in prison, or a yellowing copy of the missing poster. Bev had followed the stories when college-aged girls began disappearing from campuses, and when four-year-old Heidi Peterson disappeared from her front yard in Seattle during the same period.

Bev's closest friends and her relatives said she didn't talk about Ann. Yvonne Doherty and husband traveled with Bev and Don to Yugoslavia, and on cruises to the Caribbean and South China Sea. They met regularly with other friends for potlucks. "We were very, very good acquaintances for many decades," Doherty said. "But we didn't talk a lot about marital problems, men you wished you had married, or even missing children. None of us wanted to push the issue. A lot of our generation don't talk about these things."

Don's jealousy of Bev and need for control went with them, wherever they traveled. If she dared speak to any man, even a tour guide or a baggage handler, he would berate Bev for hours. When they were stranded in Russia, and once when their luggage was lost in Egypt, Don nagged at her for hours after she tried to help. In photographs of trips or holidays at home, there is no affection between them. "I never did see them hold hands," said Doherty. Raleigh Burr said he "never saw unbridled laughter, joy, mirth" between Bev and his brother.

Bev's mother, Marie, seemed to begrudge Bev's freedom to travel. She would ask her daughter, "What if I die when you're gone?" Bev would reply, "That would be too bad."

The Burrs often hosted gatherings but there was a manic quality to Bev's entertaining. Parties and holidays had to be kept light. There were games, songs, more games. At the same time Bev was "putting herself in harm's way," according to Raleigh Burr. Bev was injured in a series of accidents: she stepped on gardening shears and her shoe filled up with blood; she fell in the yard; she burned her arm. Were they self-inflicted? Dr. Conte said Bev was "acting out." "She may have felt that she doesn't deserve to be loved," Raleigh said. "She was difficult to be around—anxious, constant anxiety, she was protective of Mary," said her sister-in-law, Bonnie Taschler.

At one point, Bev was hospitalized. Julie visited her, but never knew if her mother had tried to harm herself or had experienced a breakdown. Bev told Julie that she "needed a rest." And then Bev decided she wanted to become a nun. Bev talked to her parish about the possibility of going into a convent. They discouraged her. "We were teens," Julie remembered. "It felt very confusing to know our mom wanted to leave us and become a nun. Poor mom."

In a few years, Laura would witness her mother shoplifting. Bev spent a night in jail. A counselor told Bev she was taking things because something had been taken from her.

It began with the outburst Raleigh Burr remembers. By age 12, Mary was angry, sullen, and remote, and it worsened. At first her parents thought it was just teenage behavior. Mary was sleeping a lot and stopped going to school. The school told Bev that when Mary did attend, she created a "disturbance" in class. Despite the problems in their marriage, Bev and Don were united when it came to helping their daughter. Yet, Don must have second-guessed Bev when Mary was first ill. In a short story for her community college writing class, Bev wrote about a family with a schizophrenic daughter. The husband (named Frank) criticizes his wife (Eva) because he believes the girl isn't sick; he says she is spoiled. Even Eva's son tells her she is "too nice" to his sister, that she needs to "get tough." The daughter in the story, named Mary, has stopped eating, going to school, and bathing, and has been cutting herself out of family photos. For a while, Eva is in denial, convinced that Mary only suffers from some kind of nutritional deficiency.

> *"Frank said she was defying me again, acting like a real smartie. He thought I knew how to handle an eighteen-year-old. After all, he said, I had been a schoolteacher, spent lots of money to learn those things. He claimed he didn't have nearly the trouble with her I did.*
>
> *Mary and I walked toward the car. Maple trees were budding in the front yard, [the] warm sunshine was comforting. If Mary had a vitamin deficiency affecting her nerves, Dr. Kenney could remedy the situation quickly."*

In the story, the psychiatrist admits Mary to a hospital and orders the family not to have any contact with her. "My God, she's got him fooled, too," Frank says of the compassion the doctor shows to Mary.

But it wasn't until after Mary—the real Mary—started a fire that burned a part of the house on North 20th Street and told Bev that the devil had told her to stop going to school, that Bev looked for help. She found it in Dr. William Conte, a psychiatrist in Tacoma who had once been director of the Department of Institutions for the state of Washington, including its maximum security prison at Walla Walla. Considered a "liberal social psychiatrist," Conte instituted prison reforms, culminating in what the *New York Times* called "perhaps the strangest" prison social structure in the U.S. It was the first time guards and convicts were called "corrections officers" and "residents." Inmates could grow beards, there were no uniforms, and guards were encouraged to "take a lifer home for dinner." Conte resigned in June, 1971, as the experiment began to go bad. The residents had wrested too much control; gang activity increased and inmates threatened to stage sit-downs or even take hostages if they didn't get their way. Gary Ridgway (Ted's "Riverman") is incarcerated at Walla Walla, but the lifers don't get to go out for dinner anymore.

By the time Bev sought him out, Conte had returned to private practice in Tacoma. Conte diagnosed Mary as paranoid schizophrenic. Oddly, Conte didn't tell Bev and Don directly of his diagnosis; he wrote it on a piece of paper and sealed it in an envelope, then handed it to Bev. In that pre-computer age, she was to take it to the Washington State Department of Social and Health Services herself, where the staff would help the family navigate Mary's care, including institutionalization. Naturally, Bev opened the envelope. In the short story, Eva does the same thing. Later, she asks the psychiatrist why he didn't share his diagnosis with the parents. The doctor tells her, "Because none of us at the hospital knew enough about it to be encouraging or discouraging." Dr. Conte told Bev he didn't want Mary to have to carry a "label" of schizophrenia.

Bev described Mary's diagnosis as the culmination of several years of "nightmare happenings." But what followed was worse. Many times Mary was homeless. She prostituted herself, used drugs, and showed up for Julie's wedding drunk, her bridesmaid dress soiled and smelly. Bev and Don would leave family events, even Christmas with the other children and grandchildren, to bail Mary out of jail. Laura remembered feeling both relieved and guilty that Mary wasn't at her wedding. But then Don and Bev left it early to run to Mary's rescue. Mary lost her teeth and part of an intestine, and was beaten up more than once by a boyfriend. She gave birth to a baby with severe congenital defects. She had a second child and gave both up for adoption. She married, and divorced, two fellow schizophrenics.

Bev loved her daughter, but saw her for what she was, too. She called her a "zombie," but in the next breath would soften and refer to her as "the poor little thing." Mary finally found some stability when she married a man many years her senior.

Julie resented the time and attention her parents gave to Mary's illness. Like the family members in Bev's short story, Julie wondered if her parents were enabling Mary. At the same time, Julie admired her mother's determination. "She never gave up on Mary—not for a day," Julie said. And Julie often quoted something Bev said: "I've already lost one daughter; I'm not going to lose another."

As young children, Julie, Greg, and Mary had worried that they might be kidnapped, like their sister was. Now, they worried if they, too, might become ill.

Bev, Julie, and Laura considered writing a book about schizophrenia. Julie discovered her mother was a superb researcher. The three each made notes of their memories, in order to tell the story of a family with a schizophrenic daughter and sister from different points of view.

Bev wrote of difficulties surrounding Mary's birth.

> *"Neighbors called to find out why I'm still without a baby. What happened? Just late, I said. She was due on Thanksgiving, her cousin near Christmas, but Mary came Dec. 19 and the cousin at Thanksgiving. Everybody at home was ready for Christmas, and when are we going to be home? Mary wouldn't eat; finally released us Dec. 24 when her weight reached 5 pounds again. No preschools existed then but you had fun hiking with your family from the time you were about 3. But then your sister, who held you on her lap and looked at picture books with*

you, being the oldest and wisest in your opinion, was kidnapped from our home. You were the last person to see beloved Ann. How afraid were you from then on? How afraid were all of us with police in the basement every day, recording all messages, hoping... "

Julie and Laura's memories were about Mary setting the house on fire, running away from home, stealing from her sisters, and her hallucinations. Julie had never forgotten how the children were taken along to help search for their sister Ann. They apparently were taken to visit Mary in the psychiatric ward, too. Laura wrote:

"I don't think I should have gone there. I don't think it was appropriate.

I feel I was too young to comprehend... or maybe just not informed enough from my parents. Mary was absolutely psycho hitting the door to get out of her room, screaming that there was poison or something coming out of her lights. She cut off all her hair. It was totally out of control and I should not have witnessed this."

It was confusing for Julie. She admired her parents for not giving up on Mary, but resented some of their choices.

"One time mom and dad stayed with my three kids while Marco and I went on vacation. Mary and her abusive husband were in jail. Mom and dad took my three young children to the jail somewhere down south to bail them out. I was scared for my kids and felt it very inappropriate to expose little children to that scene. Another

*time when mom and dad were babysitting... they allowed Mary and another of her bizarre husbands to come over, again a decision I resented. I did not want them at my house as they were drug addicts, dealers, thiefs [*sic*], etc. Somehow they broke my plastic yard furniture. Oh well. Worse, mom told me Mary had slept in my bed and that she had crabs. Disgusting."*

Dr. Conte advised Bev and Don to not let Mary live at home, and dozens of times Bev and Don and the other kids would help Mary get settled in a new apartment. Then she would be evicted, her things stolen, and the process would start again. Julie tried to help Mary by visiting her, buying her clothes and taking her to lunch, trying desperately to understand the way Mary thought.

"One time she couldn't wait until her latest boyfriend was released from jail. About two days after he was released, he overdosed and died. I told her I was sorry and she said something like, 'oh well.' "

It reminded Julie of Mary's "blasé attitude" when she almost burned the house down.

It was only at her sickest that Mary may have started to have memories or dreams of Ann. Hospitalized at St. Joseph Medical Center in Tacoma, Mary wrote a little each day in a running letter that she eventually sent to her parents. It was 1976 and Ted Bundy had gotten into Mary's mind; it's unclear if Mary is writing about the on-going search in the Pacific Northwest for the handsome, mysterious, still-at-large serial killer only known as "Ted," or if she knows Ted Bundy, a local boy, has been convicted of kidnapping in Utah. It would be years before he would be connected to the disappearance of Ann Marie Burr. Mary wrote:

> *"Memories of Anne [*sic*] and my room flashed, slicing through my mind a dark creature with black hair, a flash light in hand, a girl, an indian beautiful standing—I remember, quick quiet motions. Ann's hands moving, screamed covered, mine cut off by a glance and a nod, the girl safely backing out of the picture. I fainted-shock. I was made a gifted child for life under the kidnapers fight against the devil. He must have been somekind a smart man or hypnotist, pshychologist, he knew how not to wake anyone up. I must have heard him come in because through all those flash cameras I remember one in particular talking to someone behind him glancing back, me neeling calling him a [illegible] then a blank stare at the window in which they come in, the [illegible] glanced back she must have been a wake, which at that time, I must have had that feeling by Gods love for mankind, that something would happen in that night. A truck was used for they needed to rip off a few things from our home.*
>
> *The front door was left unlocked wide open, as if in later years [illegible] kidnapping Anne would reappear, and supposingly be the create crime of the century. I want that Ted locked up—death penalty. He's insane, with so much hate inside he must have the mentality of a 3 year old. What a fool, by making me the fool, you're crazy Ted. That's all I have to say—Everyone's becoming afraid by you—lay off for awhile, if you want me to kill you—Or do you*

want to live? Either way your dead! So get out of my Life Ted."

Mary ended the letter to her parents by mentioning the novel she was reading while locked away and receiving treatment. It was Ken Kesey's *One Flew Over the Cuckoo's Nest.*

In the mid-1990s, Bev received a telephone call from a psychiatrist (not her friend Dr. William Conte). He had a patient, he said, who believed she was Ann Marie. "It was like opening up a wound," according to Julie. Bev baked an apple pie and invited the woman over. "I took one look at her and knew it wasn't her," Bev said, "but she was so determined that she was Ann." The woman remembered having a canary and a few other details. Bev and Don visited with the woman five or six times. Finally, Julie encouraged her parents to do a DNA test. "I said, 'Mom, you've got to find out if it's her.'"

It took two years, but Bev and Don eventually had themselves and the woman tested. The woman was not Ann, but Bev kept a couple of photographs of her in an album.

In 1999, 38 years after their daughter vanished, Bev and Don Burr held a memorial mass for Ann. There were numerous articles in the Tacoma and Seattle newspapers revisiting the case and the possible Ted Bundy connection. By then, Bev was glad that she didn't know what had happened to Ann. "I still think it was someone she knew," she concluded. But she was glad she didn't know the details of how Ann died. "You know, he tortured women," she said of Ted Bundy.

In one of the newspaper articles Don was asked why they were finally having a service. "Life's cycle is coming around," he said, "and we think we may want to finish this and face the reality of one of our children who has left us." Don was not well, and he and Bev thought the memorial mass was the last chance for someone to come forward with information about what happened to Ann.

More than 200 friends and family attended. The current priest at St. Patrick's—Bev thought he looked like actor Richard Gere—led the prayers and someone played a piano piece Ann had been practicing when she disappeared. Tony Zatkovich spoke about getting to know the Burr family and trying to solve the case. As he always did, he spoke his mind. When the retired detective started to go into a little too much detail about the person he suspected of taking Ann, someone gently interrupted him and escorted him from the lectern.

Bev and Don didn't speak at the service, but Julie did. "You probably wanted to crawl into bed and bury your head as each day and year passed with no answer. But instead you gathered strength and provided us with a wonderful childhood," she said.

The Burrs planted a tree in front of St. Patrick's in Ann's memory. Ann Rule sent the family an azalea that lived for years thanks to Bev's green thumb. Bev kept a photograph of it in an album.

13
The Blue House

ON AUGUST 31, 2008, 47 YEARS TO THE DAY AFTER her daughter disappeared, Beverly Burr dragged the hose connecting her to her oxygen from her living room, through the kitchen, out the backdoor, and down the steps to her patio, nearly tripping as the tubing got tangled under her feet. Her determination—which had seen her through a lonely childhood, a lonely marriage, the abduction of her first born, and the heartbreak of a schizophrenic daughter—was still evident.

Bev was 80 years old, dying of congestive heart failure, and too ill to garden.

But she loved being outdoors and would sit in her canopy patio swing, usually with a magazine and her huge cat, Thomas, nicknamed "Stinky Poo," nearby. Thomas was devoted to her but had recently scratched her and drawn blood from her gaunt arms. It didn't bother Bev. She didn't even apply a bandage. She still went to the trouble of putting bobby pins in her hair, and she still forgot to take them out.

Bev had not lost her acerbic sense of humor. Against her wishes, her children paid a neighbor to check on her twice a day, "in order to see if I'm dead," she deadpanned. She left the back door unlocked for the woman, and joked that she was "taking the risk of being stabbed to death" in her home. And everywhere—on a kitchen counter, held by a magnet to the refrigerator, and on a coffee table—were notes imploring the person who found her ill or dead to *not* call an ambulance or rush her to a hospital. There were also notes reminding them not to forget Thomas. Earlier that summer, a visitor was present when a hospice doctor stopped by. The doctor examined her, talked with her a bit and told Bev that she had about two months to live. While his back was turned, she looked at the visitor and rolled her eyes as she often did to indicate just how seriously (or not) she took things.

During that visit, she told the hospice doctor—who she hadn't met before, and who had no idea who she was or what sorrows she had faced—that her heart had been through a lot. She told him that one of her daughters had been abducted and never found, and another had schizophrenia. It was a rare admission of heartache. And she repeated, as she so often had over the years, "I never cry because I'll never quit."

Bev hated the blue-violet color of the house on North Proctor. In fact, she felt her children had rushed the decision to leave her home on North 28th, the house with the huge yard and the view of Commencement Bay. That house represented life after Ann. It was where she gardened for neighbors who paid her without Don knowing. Among her neighbors were Ted Strand's son and Robert Bruzas, Tony Zatkovich's favorite suspect in the disappearance of Ann. The homes of Strand and Bruzas overlooked the Burr home. Strand remembers his father visiting with Bruzas in his driveway.

Bev's children prevailed on her to move after she broke an ankle and had “a heart episode” at Thanksgiving. Julie, Greg, and Laura found the blue house and packed her up and moved her. Among the items Bev finally gave away were the jumper and blouse she had bought Ann to wear the first day of third grade, and the doll with the blue and white nightgown that matched Ann's. Bev threw away the many lists she had kept of people who had telephoned or written the family about Ann's disappearance, including the famous and not-so-famous psychics, the dowsers, the mentally ill, and the well-intentioned. Bev made sure she would still have the same phone number at the blue house, the one she'd always had, the one Ann would know.

The plan was that since Bev had never learned to drive, the move to the blue house would give her a neighborhood to walk to. It was close to shops in the Proctor District, including grocery stores, the used book store, and the movie theater. “She was finally free, free to live her life the way she wanted to live,” said Bonnie Taschler. But she almost immediately become ill and life at the blue house went downhill from there.

By 2008, Bev Burr was ready to die. She didn't want to create a fuss for her children. To the end of her life, she enjoyed reading, watching movies on

DVDs (but not the foreign films one friend brought her), and *Judge Judy* every afternoon. She followed the news of the world's latest missing child, four-year-old Madeleine McCann, who vanished on a trip to Portugal. Bev suspected the parents of foul play.

Life hadn't been easy at times for her children and grandchildren. There had been depression, alcoholism, arrests. Julie Burr described the family she grew up in as "dysfunctional, which probably began with Ann's disappearance." She is still fearful of the dark and of being home alone. A relative says that not only was Julie's life changed by her sister's abduction, but having another sister who is schizophrenic was "a huge burden." A mother of three, the usual parental worries—such as a child who disappears for an instant in a store—are more acute for Julie. But if the last 50 years have left her with a fear of the dark, they have also instilled in her an empathy for others who suffer tragedies. And the baby Bev and Don adopted two years after Ann disappeared—Laura—is Julie's salvation. Bev was happy about the closeness between Julie and Laura.

Some of Ted Bundy's boyhood friends did not fare well. There was alcoholism and drug addiction. One close childhood friend reportedly tried to kill his wife and children. Families became estranged. Some have changed their name and left Tacoma behind. Others have lived normal lives, except that Ted Bundy has remained a looming presence in their lives. A relative of Ted's says he "ruined" his mother's life. As for Louise's other children and grandchildren, Ted's sister, Linda Bussey, said: "Can you imagine what it is like for people with the name Bundy? "

Sandi Holt, who as a young girl followed her brother Doug and his best friend, Ted Bundy, everywhere, has been disabled with a debilitating disease since her twenties. A twice-divorced mother of three, she lives alone in low-income housing. Her memories of Ann Marie Burr, who she knew from riding their bicycles, and of the boy who abused animals, Ted Bundy, are clear and strong. Sandi hasn't spoken with her brother in more than 25 years. She limited contact with her father, too. According to her stepmother, her father finally grasped the pain he had inflicted when he sexually abused his children and their friends. As he was dying, C__ Holt would pace the floor late at night and cry out, "Oh, Sandi, what did I do to you? "

Bev outlived almost everyone who was a part of the story of Ann's disappearance.

Donald F. Burr, Tacoma's noted architect, well-respected for his design of many homes, schools and businesses, died in 1982 at age 60. He never quit believing that his daughter, Debra Sue, was the intended kidnap victim on August 31, 1961.

Former Chief of Detectives Bob Drost—the only member of the police force who believed Ann Marie Burr was still alive—died in 1984. He had described the investigation and lack of clues as "a handful of nothing... like grabbing at clouds." His wife said that before he died he had changed his mind and believed that Ted Bundy had killed Ann.

George Voigt, Marie Leach's second husband and Bev's father's cousin, died in 1986. Marie lived to be 95 years old. The story Bev liked to tell—about how her mother slipped on ice cream, lay on the floor for a few hours, and later died—occurred in 1994.

Larry M__, the man who had loved Bev and wanted her to call off her marriage to Don, died in 1995. He had been a well-respected insurance agent in Tacoma, a lodge member, a husband, father, and grandfather. Years later, when Bev was moving to the blue house, Julie found Larry's obituary. "She apparently treasured it, and had it hidden on her shelf in her bedroom under some knickknack," Julie said.

Ted Strand died in 1997 following heart surgery. He had smoked for 55 years. After retirement, he and Tony Zatkovich met at least once a week for lunch and to talk about the only major case they never solved. "He was a hell of a cop," Zatkovich told the *News Tribune* after Strand's death.

Richard Raymond McLish, the habitual car thief who claimed to have wrapped Ann in a quilt and buried her in an Oregon bean field, died in 2000. The native American had spent much of his adult life in the Oklahoma State Penitentiary. A brief obituary mentioned his "smile and constant willingness to help."

Tony Zatkovich not only outlived his best friend and his partner on the force, he outlived his ex-wife and his second wife. He died in 2004, just days before he turned 91. He had gone back to the police department one last time and asked to see the Ann Marie Burr file, case #176685. At least half of it was missing. He was furious. "It killed dad," Dick Zatkovich says of the sorrow his father felt over not solving the case. Bev added the newspaper obituaries for both detectives to her albums.

Don Burr died in 2003 at age 78. His illness leading up to his death was hard on Bev. Bonnie Taschler once asked Bev if she and Don had grown closer before he died. "We shed a lot of tears," Bev told her. Bev also told her that she "had always loved someone else." Bev and Don were married 52 years.

Johnnie Bundy died in 2007. He had been married to Louise for 56 years. His obituary said he was the father of five, grandfather of six, and great-grandfather of 15. None of his children were mentioned by name, including his most famous son. Ted's grandfather, Samuel Cowell, died while Ted was on death row. Louise told a reporter that she didn't know how much her father knew about his grandson's crimes. One family member says they hid newspaper articles from Cowell. Louise said the family just never talked about it.

There was less chance now that Bev Burr and Louise Bundy would run into each other at a grocery store or on a bus trip. Bev—who had vowed never to move to an apartment or to senior citizen housing because she wouldn't be able to garden—was trapped in her house. Louise would soon move from her home on North 20th into an assisted living facility. Did she keep albums and scrapbooks, as Bev did, in order to try and comprehend what happened to her first born? In preparation for Louise's move, her daughter said the family had finally destroyed letters and newspaper articles Louise and Johnnie had saved over the years. Louise Bundy was 88 when she died in December, 2012.

Bev had regrets. She regretted that she taught her children to trust people. She regretted that she didn't let Ann sleep at a friend's house that August night and that she sent her two daughters upstairs to bed alone. She regretted sleeping through Ann's abduction. She regretted that she didn't become a writer and couldn't love Don enough. And she had secrets. Why did she continue to say that she had been a "terrible person?" Was she, as some family members believed, just being dramatic? Or did she blame herself for her daughter's disappearance? Bev internalized the pain and grief she carried for years. It bled from her when she cut blackberry bushes, shoplifted, and was so desperate to change her life that she would have left her family for a convent.

After Ann vanished, Bev started Julie in religious education classes and moved her to the school at St. Patrick's. Julie didn't want to leave Grant Elementary School where she was in second grade and Ann was supposed to have been in third. "I remember thinking my mom made us convert and change schools because she felt she was being punished from God for not following her Catholic beliefs. I'm not sure how I arrived at that." In a newspaper article in 1963, around the time of Laura's adoption, Bev implied that God hadn't been listening to her prayers.

Grief experts say that guilt stops the healing process, and ambiguous loss—the kind without a body to bury and mourn—is the most devastating kind because it is incomplete. The greater the ambiguity, the greater the anxiety, depression, and family stress. Some people survive loss by clinging to denial and hope. Louise Bundy did. But Bev, who knew from the early moments of August 31, 1961, that she would never see her daughter again, only pretended to have hope. She pretended for the newspapers, for her other children, and probably for Ann. Bev never romanticized Ann's homecoming. She was incapable of living in denial and was the worst for it. Ayn Rand wrote, "Guilt is a rope that wears thin." Bev's rope wore very thin.

Beverly Burr died in her home on North Proctor Street on September 13, 2008. The notes imploring those who loved her not to call an ambulance or take her to the hospital and not to forget about her cat Thomas were still on the counter and the refrigerator. Her wishes were honored. Her children, except for Mary, spent time with her at the end of her life. She was the mother of five, grandmother of seven, and great-grandmother of three.

Bev remained ambiguous about her Catholic faith. She pretended it was a comfort, but didn't depend on it. The week she died one of her caregivers left a religious pamphlet at Bev's bedside. If Bev read it, it might have provided solace. It read: God uses ordinary people to do extraordinary work.

14
Explaining Ted

TRYING TO EXPLAIN TED IS NOT EXPLAINING AWAY Ted, or forgiving him. Regardless of what childhood or genetic influences shaped him, he does not deserve sympathy. To the end of his life he was without remorse and his words for his victims and their families still have the power to shock. "What's one less person on the face of the earth, anyway?" he remarked when discussing his crimes. Ted went so far as to tell former investigator Bob Keppel that there were people who deserved to be raped and murdered.

When Ted told psychiatrist Dr. Dorothy Otnow Lewis that everyone else wanted to know *what* he did, but she was the only one who wanted to know *why,* he was correct. Police in at least six states and the FBI were desperate to know when he started killing, how he lured his victims, how many girls and women he killed, where he disposed of their bodies, and if he was responsible for other missing women and unsolved crimes. Dr. Lewis, and now another generation of researchers, hope to better understand the minds of serial killers. They are convinced murderers are made, not born.

If Ted Bundy was on death row today, we'd know a lot more about him. Until the 1980s, the study of the causes of crime focused on socio-economic factors, including poverty. When Dr. Lewis first met Ted in 1986, she was in the middle of conducting research on juveniles condemned to death. In one of her studies, she compared juveniles on death row to incarcerated delinquents who did not commit violent offenses. She found the juveniles on death row had been physically abused as children; they had a mental illness; they had a close relative who was mentally ill; they committed violent acts during childhood; and there was neurological impairment caused by a head injury.

Do all children who are abused, or are bipolar, or sustain a head injury, grow up to be killers? No, but they are predictors of future violence if a young person suffers from all three.

About the same time Dr. Lewis was conducting her research, Canadian psychologist Robert Hare was deep into his study of psychopaths. Building on the work of Dr. Hervey Checkley in the 1940s, Hare developed the PCLR (Psychopath Checklist-Revised) a clinical rating scale used to assess psychopathy. What Checkley called insincerity, Hare called glibness and superficial charm. Also on his list of psychopathic traits are: a grandiose sense of self-worth; pathological lying; conning and manipulation of others; lack of a conscience; lack of remorse or guilt; an overall shallow affect; callousness and lack of empathy; failure to accept responsibility for one's actions; impulsivity; juvenile delinquency; tendency to boredom; and early behavioral problems. Studies of unattached children, children who haven't bonded with the parental figures in their life, have their own checklist, a kind of junior version of Hare's checklist. It includes cruelty to others; phoniness; speech pathology; preoccupation with fire, blood or gore; and pathological lying. There is little doubt that Ted today would be considered by many to be a psychopath. Dr. Lewis doesn't use psychopathy as a diagnosis and considers its definition "loose." Other psychiatrists share her concern.

But if this is how a psychopath behaves, how did he get that way? (And it is almost always a "he"—female psychopaths are much rarer.)

Dr. Kent Kiehl grew up in Tacoma sitting around the dinner table talking about Ted Bundy's crimes with his father, an editor for the Tacoma News Tribune. Now an associate professor of psychology and neuroscience at the University of New Mexico, Dr. Kiehl is scanning the brains of a thousand inmates a year at 12 state prisons to learn more about the roots of psychopathy. Dr. Kiehl, who studied with Robert Hare, said there is no evidence that a traumatic childhood (including molestation), or a traumatic head injury, make someone a killer. Instead, he is focusing on abnormalities he has found in their paralimbic systems, the network of brain regions involved in processing emotions and inhibitions. Kiehl hopes that, someday, there will be a drug that targets the region of the brain involved.

Several studies are looking at the possibility of a genetic component to psychopathy (which was also known as sociopathy, and now is used interchangeably with antisocial personality disorder). Even Ted suggested that he might have inherited a genetic predisposition to aggressive behavior. If he had donated his brain to science, as Dr. Lewis hoped he would, who knows what secrets might have been revealed.

Other studies of what is called "a high-risk gene," a variant of the MAOA gene associated with violence, indicate that, combined with child abuse, the gene "increases one's chances of being convicted of a violence offense by more than 400 percent."

An FBI study found that childhood experiences are critical to understanding serial killers. The 2002 study found that animal abuse is an important predictor of future violence. So is family dysfunction. Nearly 70 percent of the convicts the FBI looked at came from families with alcohol-abuse. Fifty percent had been severely beaten; some had been sexually abused; many had family members with criminal histories; and three quarters reported "psychological" abuse, which includes indifference. In most cases, early "bizarre behavior" by children was ignored by their families.

What does not appear on the lists of predictors is pornography. Ted Bundy liked to warn America about pornography and the influence of the media. He told James Dobson, in the infamous video interview taped the night before he was executed: "I've met a lot of men who were motivated to commit violence just like me. And without exception, without question, every one of them was deeply involved in pornography." Bob Keppel, Ann Rule, Stephen Michaud and others thought Ted was grandstanding. Experts say pornography may shape fantasies, but it doesn't make someone a serial killer.

Studies of head injuries now extend to former professional football players. Twenty NFL veterans have been found to have the same trauma-induced brain disease, chronic traumatic encephalopathy (CTE), a progressive degenerative disease caused by multiple concussions and other forms of head injury. Once found mostly in boxers, its symptoms can include a deteriorating mental state, memory loss, depression, dementia, as well as poor impulse control and abusive behavior.

The first time Ted had a mental examination was when he was awaiting trial for the kidnapping of Carol DaRonch. A University of Utah clinical psychologist spent two hours with Ted and administered six tests, including a Rorschach and the Minnesota Multiphasic Personality Inventory exam. Ted was vehemently denying his guilt, and the psychologist stated that he was forced to conclude that Ted was a "normal person." Later, after being found guilty, Ted was given a more extensive evaluation. Still at Utah State Prison, Ted participated in 50 hours of tests. During a skull X-ray a small benign tumor was discovered in his left sinus passage. An electroencephalogram (or EEG), which measures electrical activity in the brain was "completely unremarkable," and doctors found "no evidence of organic brain disease." However, a prison psychiatrist did determine that Ted had an "anti-social personality," including a lack of guilt feelings, callousness, rationalization, withdrawn and other factors "consistent with a schizoid personality." (Not related to schizophrenia, schizoid suggests an aloof, cold and indifferent personality.) There was also a scar on his scalp. Other tests, administered when Ted was on death row in Florida, found a "slightly abnormal" EEG; an intelligence test showed an "extraordinary gap" between his verbal I.Q. and his poor ability to see spatial relationships, something Dr. Lewis says can be a dysfunction of the central nervous system. According to the FBI, the autopsy of his brain found no abnormalities, but experts say it would not necessarily have detected a neuropsychological dysfunction (such as bipolar disease). The postmortem also noted the scar on his scalp; there's no way of knowing if it dated from childhood, from a 1973 ski accident, or had any significance.

Ted knew there was something wrong. He told his longtime girlfriend, "There is something the matter with me." He called himself a vampire, because of how much he enjoyed his late night roaming.

And those around him—at least those not in denial—saw abnormal behavior from the time he was young. He arranged the knives around his teenage aunt to scare her. Sandi Holt saw him drag little girls into the woods and urinate on them. He abused animals, and Holt saw his eyes change as his irises darkened. His friends saw sudden outbursts of rage. His grade school teachers said he had trouble controlling his temper. He hit a friend on the head with a stick.

His great-aunt witnessed Ted in "an altered state." An investigator for the Florida public defender said he twice saw Ted "turn into another person," right in front of him. During these episodes Ted's skin changed color, he emitted a strange odor, and he became incoherent. Michaud and Aynesworth noticed how close together his eyes appeared sometimes. Attorney Polly Nelson said that when Ted described a murder he committed in Idaho, he went into a "trance" and said he had experienced "frenzies" when killing.

Ted came close to having a multiple personality disorder. Now called Dissociative Identity Disorder, it is thought to be a coping mechanism to help a person dissociate himself from memories of an experience that are too traumatic to deal with consciously. At its most severe, it causes multiple personalities. A person with multiple personalities is usually unaware of their other selves. Ted always seemed aware of what he sometimes called "the entity" or "the other Ted." He told Nelson that he heard "the other Ted" talking to him, and the cycle of drinking, stalking a victim, and committing murder would begin. Ted told Dr. Lewis: "And I'm not saying that I was a multiple personality. I don't know. All I know is that this other part of myself seemed to have a voice, and seemed to have a need." He went on to tell her that he was "not totally unconscious of, or unaware" of the "entity," but he was in some kind of altered state at those times.

Those who knew Ted are still trying to understand how he became a man that even *he* said society should be protected from.

"I've never gone for the 'bad seed' theory, but I do believe you can have a predisposition to killing," Ann Rule said. And she believes that a combination of a predisposition to violence and abuse can cause some kind of psychological break.

Dr. Ron Holmes, the serial killer researcher Ted "confessed" the abduction and murder of Ann Marie Burr to, said it is natural to want to find a cause, whether it is genes or brain damage. "But we're only studying the people who get caught," he said. "There are some (psychopaths) who never get into trouble, so the sample is skewed. The only thing they have in common is an overwhelming compulsion to kill. Where it arises from, I don't know." Holmes' theory is that something happens early in childhood, probably a head injury. "There's just something about these people, they are wired differently and have an overarching need to kill."

Bob Keppel, the former King County detective who led the search for Ted in the 1970s, later earned a Ph.D. in Criminal Justice from the University of Washington. He discounts the stories about childhood abuse and what role Ted's grandfather had in shaping Ted's psychopathy. Keppel called the story about Ted putting knives around his aunt, "a bunch of garbage." He had interviewed Ted's east coast family, too, and never heard that story or others about what went on at Ted's grandfather's house. And he doesn't believe that Ted turned into an “entity” at times. “What I have learned mostly is, serial killers are all different. My guess is he killed because he liked it. It is not about chromosomes.”

Ted's sister, Linda Bussey, will only say she has “no idea, no clue” what made him the way he was. She won’t hypothesize about mental illness, or his diagnosis of bipolar disease. “That is not the person I knew,” is all she will say.

Dr. Lewis has not yet completed her analysis of the hours she spent with Ted Bundy. Lewis said she tried to get Ted to talk about things he had never talked about, but that he was ashamed of something. She has said that his last words to her were about how he felt unloved by his mother, and the anger that caused. As a young man he had been embarrassed by his illegitimacy. Is that a clue to his rage? In the film version of Ann Rule's *The Stranger Beside Me*, the character of Ted Bundy is being assessed by a prison psychiatrist. Pressed to try and explain what made him kill dozens of women and girls, Ted says, “I don’t like being humiliated.”

Or maybe the reason is as simple as what Ted once told FBI agent Bill Hagmaier: *“I just liked to kill. I wanted to kill.”*

15

What Happened to Ann Marie Burr?

SALESMEN NO LONGER GO DOOR-TO-DOOR IN NORTH Tacoma selling pots and pans or plans for backyard bomb shelters. Gusty's orchard, next to the Burr house, is gone; an apartment complex stands on the lot. The fraternities and dorms under construction at the University of Puget Sound in 1961 are showing their age. The areas that were deep ditches that summer are now just well-used city streets. Ann Marie Burr is probably entombed under one of them.

There were a few suspects, but no arrest. Tacoma police questioned thousands of people and gave polygraphs to hundreds of them during the Ann Marie Burr investigation. The leading suspects included the teenage neighbor boy who flirted with Ann; Ann's cousin who grew up to be a child molester; and the two bean pickers from Oregon looking for work. Another was the traveling salesman who liked to take young girls for rides in his convertible. Police didn't yet know the teenager from across town who was already experienced at peeping in windows, animal abuse, stealing, and scaring little girls.

Complicating the search for Ann was the dearth of clues: there were no witnesses, no physical evidence at the crime scene (according to the police report), no vehicle description or license plate, no fingerprints, no credible ransom demand, no motive, no weapon, no burial site, and no body. There was a footprint, and a single red thread. There may be no direct physical evidence linking Ted Bundy, or anybody else, to the disappearance of Ann Marie Burr, but as police say, absence of evidence is not the same as evidence of absence.

In August, 2011 the FBI announced it had added Ted Bundy's DNA to a national databank in hopes it might solve some cold cases or eliminate him as a suspect in murders he has been tied to over the years. It used a vial of his blood drawn in 1978 when he was arrested in connection with the murder of 12-year old Kimberly Diane Leach. Julie Burr was asked to give a sample of her DNA to Tacoma police. Police say Ted Bundy's DNA did not match any items saved from the Burr house.

For more than five years, detectives Ted Strand and Tony Zatkovich worked to solve the case. After they retired, they spent another 30 years doing what they did best—talking it through. It was how they had solved hundreds of other crimes. They were still trying to solve the disappearance of Ann Marie Burr when they died.

What nearly everyone agreed on—50 years ago and today—is that Ann Marie Burr probably knew the person who took her, and is most likely buried somewhere nearby.

Detective Tony Zatkovich said that the Ann Burr case was the only one he and Ted Strand ever disagreed on. In a *News Tribune* article published in September, 1999, at the time of the family's memorial service for Ann, Zatkovich said, "Bundy had absolutely nothing to do with this. He was a real murderer and one of the worst, but he didn't have anything to do with this."

But Ted Bundy's hypothetical confession before he was executed has gained credibility over the years. In the same story where Zatkovich discounts Ted as a suspect, Tacoma Detective Larry Lindberg, described as "currently assigned to the Burr case," (missing child cases are never closed), was quoted as saying the police "are pretty sure Bundy was the killer." In 2010, Tacoma police homicide detective Lindsey Wade took over the cold case.

Zatkovich's favorite suspect remained Robert Bruzas, the 15-year-old neighbor of Ann's. He and Ann were friendly, even flirtatious. For 50 years Bruzas has lived with the knowledge that he was Zatkovich's chief suspect. "I knew that, but it doesn't bother me a bit," Bruzas said. He attributes not passing his first polygraph to nerves. "They had me scared to death," he says of his two interrogations at the hands of Zatkovich and Strand.

Detective Strand thought the best suspect was Ralph Everett Larkee, the automotive parts salesman from Spokane who in 1964 took 10-year-old Gay Lynn Stewart on a ride around the Northwest in his Buick convertible and shot himself with the FBI at his door. There's no record of why Strand was convinced that Larkee had taken Ann Burr. Maybe it was in the part of the file that is lost.

The two detectives never ruled out Richard Raymond McLish who said he and a friend had taken Ann and buried her on an Oregon farm.

Author Ann Rule is asked more often about the disappearance of Ann Marie Burr than about any other case. She believes it was Ted Bundy's first murder. "I still do think it was Ted," she said. The coincidences—that Ted had lived nearby when he and Louise first moved to Tacoma, that he was a paperboy, that his last victim was 12 years old—is more convincing than Ted's excuses that he was too young at the time and lived too far from the Burr house.

The details in his confession match the facts of the case. How did he know about the apple orchard next door, or exactly which upstairs bedroom Ann slept in? Robert Cour's article in *Master Detective* in 1966 mentioned the window being up, the door unlocked from the inside and standing open, and Don seeing what looked like a workman standing over a ditch. Had Ted read, and remembered, that story, published when he was a teenager? Or did he know the details because he was the one standing by the ditch?

Ted hypothesized to Holmes that a killer could have started at age 14 or 15 by murdering an eight- or nine-year-old girl, and said that committing a murder when young was a "mystical, exciting... overwhelming experience." And Ted told Dr. Lewis and others that *something* had happened to him when he was 14 or 15. The only other murder Ted would never discuss, even hypothetically, was his last, that of 12-year-old Kimberly Diane Leach.

Bob Keppel was the last person to ask Ted about Ann Marie Burr. It was two days before Ted was executed. "He was tired, he was frustrated, he was looking for any way to get out of the execution. It would have been [an] ideal time for him to talk about a missing victim who had not been found. It would show how he was trying to provide information," Keppel said. But by then, Ted knew that Florida's governor was not going to negotiate. Keppel said he doesn't know who killed Ann Marie Burr, but he doesn't think it was Ted Bundy. "I deal in probabilities, not possibilities," Keppel said.

Like Holmes, Keppel believes there are some victims that killers don't talk about. Ted even mentioned it. "He had indicated to me that there were crimes that serial killers would never reveal to authorities because they held a special meaning to them, such as a child, someone they knew, or someone close to home," Keppel said.

When Ted's possible involvement with the Ann Marie Burr case was resurrected at the time of her memorial mass in 1999, Louise Bundy told the *News Tribune*, "I feel so sorry for the Burr family because they've sort of latched onto this. But he couldn't have done it." Of course, the Burr family wouldn't have "latched" onto the possibility of Ted's involvement if he hadn't described his movements that morning, down to the shuffling of dirt with his feet and watching the police talk to Bev and Don.

Ted's family remains angry that he is still a suspect in the disappearance of Ann Marie Burr. His sister, Linda Bussey, called it "ancient, ancient history."

"It's disgusting, it's maddening," she said. "He had nothing to do with her disappearance. He was a young kid. People thought he was the Green River Killer, too. We might as well say he raped and murdered everyone." Ted's cousin, Edna Cowell Martin, is more pragmatic. She thinks that the fact that Ted lived a couple of miles west on Skyline Drive in 1961 makes his involvement less likely.

Ann was up and down a couple of times during the night, taking the crying Mary to their parent's room. Did Ann see someone she knew at the window during one of those trips? Did she unlock the front door for him? Or did someone familiar with the house climb through the window and enter Ann's upstairs bedroom? Was she silenced in her room or in the orchard next door? Sunrise was 6:27 that morning. Bev Burr discovered her daughter missing between 5:15 and 5:30 a.m., but Ann could have been gone for hours. If it was still dark when Ann was taken, it would only take a few minutes to take her to the orchard and then two blocks west to the UPS campus, or one block east to the sewer construction project, or put her in a car.

For four years I've studied UPS building plans, city sewer plans, researched the childhood (and adult years) of Ted Bundy, talked to dozens of people who knew him well, investigated other suspects, and spent hundreds of hours with the Burr family. I think Ted Bundy lured Ann Marie Burr out of her home and killed her. Bev Burr and Louise Bundy didn't think their children knew each other. But Sandi Holt says she knows they did—because she knew them *both.* Ann reportedly followed Ted around "like a puppy dog." Maybe Ann watched him get his newspapers ready to deliver, like she did Robert. Maybe Ted flirted with Ann, like the other neighbor boys and some of her cousins did. She was comfortable around teenagers.

I believe Ted was the prowler that the Burr's and others in the neighborhood reported seeing and hearing in the weeks leading up to Ann's disappearance. He crawled through the living room window and went up to her bedroom. Or maybe he saw Ann passing through the house with Mary that evening, leaned through the window, and asked her to open the front door. Ann, seeing his familiar face, feeling safe with him, thinking the day was beginning with an adventure, left her bedroom with him, or undid the chain lock and opened the door. Then he took her by the hand and out into the pre-dawn morning.

Ted Bundy's Victims

Unknown hitchhiker, early September, 1974 Idaho.

Lynda Ann Healy–January 31/February 1, 1974 Seattle, Washington.

Donna Gail Manson–March 12, 1974 Olympia, Washington.

Susan Rancourt–April 17, 1974 Ellensburg, Washington.

Roberta Kathleen Parks–May 6, 1974 Corvallis, Oregon.

Brenda Ball–June 1, 1974 Seattle, Washington.

Georgeann Hawkins–June 11, 1974 Seattle, Washington.

Janice Ott–July 14, 1974 Lake Sammamish, Washington.

Denise Naslund–July 14, 1974 Lake Sammamish, Washington.

Nancy Wilcox–October 2, 1974 Salt Lake City, Utah.

Melissa Smith–October 18, 1974 Salt Lake City, Utah.

Laura Aime–October 31, 1974 Salt Lake City, Utah.

Carol DaRonch (survived)–November 8, 1974 Murray, Utah.

Debra Kent–November 8, 1974 Murray, Utah.

Caryn Campbell–January 12, 1975 Snowmass, Colorado.

Julie Cunningham–March 15, 1975 Vail, Colorado.

Denise Oliverson–April 6, 1975 Grand Junction, Colorado.

Lynette Culver–May 6, 1975 Pocatello, Idaho.

Susan Curtis–June 27, 1975 Provo, Utah.

Margaret Bowman–January 15, 1978 Tallahassee, Florida.

Lisa Levy–January 15, 1978 Tallahassee, Florida.

Kathy Kleiner (survived)–January 15, 1978 Tallahassee, Florida.

Karen Chandler (survived)–January 15, 1978 Tallahassee, Florida.

Cheryl Thomas (survived)–January, 15, 1978 Tallahassee, Florida.

Kimberly Diane Leach–February 9, 1978 Lake City, Florida.

Bundy confessed to at least seven other murders which law enforcement authorities have not identified by name and have not found a body.

Data is from U.S. Department of Justice, Federal Bureau of Investigation, Ted Bundy Multiagency Investigative Team Report 1992, and other documents.

Suspected Victims

Ann Marie Burr disappeared in Tacoma, Washington, August 31, 1961.

Two United Airlines stewardesses, one killed, one survived, Seattle, Washington, June 23, 1966.

Two coeds killed at New Jersey shore, Memorial Day weekend, 1969.

Kerry May-Hardy, missing from Seattle's Capitol Hill, June, 1972 (remains found September, 2010).

Number of Victims

When he was arrested in Florida in 1978 and his killing spree was finally over, Ted Bundy intimated to police that he had killed hundreds of woman and girls.

Ted Bundy admitted to his attorney, Polly Nelson, that he had killed 30.

An FBI report stated he had killed 30 women and girls in six states, of which 20 murders were verified.

An FBI agent told Florida authorities the night before Bundy was executed that there were 50 victims.

Bundy suggested to serial killer researcher Ronald Holmes that there were more than 300 victims, including women in a total of 10 states.

Notes on Sources

Prologue

Interviews with Beverly Burr and Sandi Holt.

Tacoma Police Department, Missing Person Report on Ann Marie Burr, case #176685, August 31, 1961–October 16, 1967.

Tacoma News Tribune, Seattle Times, Seattle Post-Intelligencer.

Morgan, Murray, "Murray's People," Tacoma Public Library Northwest Room.

Chapter 1

Interviews with Ann Rule, Dorothy Otnow Lewis, Polly Nelson, and Edna Martin.

Kendall, Elizabeth, *The Phantom Prince—My Life With Ted Bundy* (Madrona Publishers: 1981).

Nelson, Polly, *Defending the Devil* (William Morrow and Company, Inc: 1994).

MacPherson, Myra, "The Roots of Evil," *Vanity Fair,* May 1989.

Magid, Ken and McKelvey, Carole A., *High Risk: Children Without A Conscience* (Bantam: 1989).

Michaud, Stephen G. and Aynesworth, Hugh, *The Only Living Witness* (Signet: 1989) and *Ted Bundy: Conversations with a Killer* (Authorlink Press: 2000).

Rule, Ann, *The Stranger Beside Me* (Penguin: 20th anniversary edition 2001).

Ascione, Frank R., "Animal Abuse and Youth Violence," U.S. Department of Justice, Office of Juvenile Justice and Delinquency Prevention, 2002.

Kivenson-Baron, Inbal, "Fearlessness in Preschoolers: An Extreme End of the Approach and Withdrawal Temperamental Dimension," University of Haifa Faculty of Education, Haifa, Israel, 2010.

Lewis, Dorothy Otnow M.D., Yeager, Catherine A. M.A., et. al., "Objective Documentation of Child Abuse and Dissociation in 12 Murderers With Dissociative Identity Disorder," *American Journal of Psychiatry*, December 1997.

Chapter 2

Interviews with: Beverly Burr, Robert Bruzas, Fran Bruzas Trierweiler, Dick Zatkovich, Ted Strand, Julie Burr, Raleigh Burr, Bonnie Taschler, Eddie Cavallo, Roland Otis, and Yvonne Doherty.

Tacoma Police Department, Missing Person Report on Ann Marie Burr, case #176685, August 31, 1961–October 16, 1967.

Tacoma News Tribune, Seattle Times, Seattle Post-Intelligencer.

Cour, Robert, "Can You Help Find Anne Marie Burr?" *Master Detective*, April, 1966.

Chapter 3

Interviews with: Beverly Burr, Julie Burr, Raleigh Burr, Bonnie Taschler, Jeff Leach, Eddie Cavallo, Dick Zatkovich, and Ted Strand.

Tacoma Police Department, Missing Person Report on Ann Marie Burr, case #176685, August 31, 1961–October 16, 1967.

Tacoma News Tribune, Seattle Times, Seattle Post-Intelligencer.

Chapter 4

Interviews with: Beverly Burr, Edna Martin, Ann Rule, Jerry Bullat, Sandi Holt, Stephen Michaud, Dorothy Otnow Lewis, Polly Nelson, Ted Strand, Michael Sullivan, and Ron Magden.

Kendall, Elizabeth, *The Phantom Prince—My Life With Ted Bundy* (Madrona Publishers: 1981).

Michaud, Stephen G. and Aynesworth, Hugh, *The Only Living Witness* (Signet: 1989) and *Ted Bundy: Conversations with a Killer* (Authorlink Press: 2000).

Morgan, Murray, "Murray's People," Tacoma Public Library Northwest Room. Morgan, Murray *Puget's Sound—A Narrative of Early Tacoma and the Southern Sound* (University of Washington Press: Columbia Northwest Classics edition 2003), and *Skid Road Seattle* (Ballantine Books: fourth printing 1973).

Nelson, Polly, *Defending the Devil* (William Morrow and Company, Inc: 1994).

MacPherson, Myra, "The Roots of Evil," *Vanity Fair,* May 1989.

Magid, Ken and McKelvey, Carole A., *High Risk: Children* Without A Conscience (Bantam: 1989). Rule, Ann, *The Stranger Beside Me* (Penguin: 20th anniversary edition 2001).

Carson, Richard, "Incredible Affairs of Dr. Boehme," *True Detective,* May, 1966.

Cour, Robert, "Can You Help Find Anne (sic) Marie Burr?" *Master Detective,* April, 1966.

McDowell, George F., "Let Me Lead You To His Grave," Startling Detective, March, 1965.

White, Hal, "Rendezvous With A Corpse," *True Detective,* February, 1961.

U.S. Department of Justice, Federal Bureau of Investigation. Ted Bundy Multiagency Investigative Team Report 1992.

Ascione, Frank R.,"Animal Abuse and Youth Violence," U.S. Department of Justice, Office of Juvenile Justice and Delinquency Prevention, 2002.

Kivenson-Baron, Inbal, "Fearlessness in Preschoolers: An Extreme End of the Approach and Withdrawal Temperamental Dimension," University of Haifa Faculty of Education, Haifa, Israel, 2010.

Lewis, Dorothy Otnow M.D., Yeager, Catherine A. M.A., et. al., "Objective Documentation of Child Abuse and Dissociation in 12 Murderers With

Dissociative Identity Disorder," *American Journal of Psychiatry*, Decem ber 1997.

Institute for Family Violence Studies, Tallahassee, FL *Competency-Based Training Manual for Animal Abuse Investigators (The Link Between Animal and Human Abuse)*, 2000.

Chapter 5

Interviews with: Beverly Burr, Betty Drost, Julie Burr, Raleigh Burr, Bonnie Taschler, Robert Bruzas, Dick Zatkovich, Ted Strand, and Eddie Cavallo.

Tacoma Police Department, Missing Person Report on Ann Marie Burr, case #176685, August 31, 1961–October 16, 1967.

Spokesman Review, Spokane Daily Chronicle, Tacoma News, Tribune, Seattle Times, Seattle Post-Intelligencer.

Tacoma History Museum, Washington State History Museum.

Chapter 6

Interviews with Beverly Burr, Julie Burr, Raleigh Burr, and Bonnie Taschler.

Tacoma Police Department, Missing Person Report on Ann Marie Burr, case #176685, August 31, 1961–October 16, 1967.

Tacoma News Tribune, Seattle Times, Seattle Post-Intelligencer.

Chapter 7

Interviews with Jerry Bullat, Sandi Holt, Dorothy Otnow Lewis, Linda Bussey, Edna Martin, Ann Rule, Stephen Michaud, and Polly Nelson.

Kendall, Elizabeth, *The Phantom Prince—My Life With Ted Bundy* (Madrona Publishers: 1981).

Larsen, Richard W., *The Deliberate Stranger* (Pocket Books: 1980).

Michaud, Stephen G. and Aynesworth, Hugh, *The Only Living Witness* (Signet: 1989) and *Ted Bundy: Conversations with a Killer* (Authorlink Press: 2000).

Nelson, Polly, *Defending the Devil* (William Morrow and Company, Inc: 1994).

Rule, Ann, *The Stranger Beside Me* (Penguin: 20th anniversary edition 2001) and *Small Sacrifices* (Penguin: 1988).

Ascione, Frank R., "Animal Abuse and Youth Violence," U.S. Department of Justice, Office of Juvenile Justice and Delinquency Prevention, 2002.

Lewis, Dorothy Otnow M.D., Yeager, Catherine A. M.A., et. al., "Objective Documentation of Child Abuse and Dissociation in 12 Murderers With Dissociative Identity Disorder," *American Journal of Psychiatry*, December 1997.

Tacoma News Tribune, Seattle Times, Seattle Post-Intelligencer.

Chapter 8

Interviews with Beverly Burr, Julie Burr, Raleigh Burr, Bonnie Taschler, Ted Strand, and Dick Zatkovich.

Tacoma Police Department, Missing Person Report on Ann Marie Burr, case #176685, August 31, 1961–October 16, 1967.

Fiset, Louis, *Camp Harmony—Seattle's Japanese Americans and the Puyallup Assembly Center* (University of Illinois Press: 2009).

Tacoma Times, Tacoma News Tribune, Seattle Times, Seattle Post-Intelligencer.

Chapter 9

Interviews with Jerry Bullat, Edna Martin, Polly Nelson, Dorothy Ot now Lewis, Julie Burr, Bob Keppel, Jerry Bullat, Ronald Holmes, Ann Rule, and Sandi Holt.

Kendall, Elizabeth, *The Phantom Prince—My Life With Ted Bundy* (Madrona Publishers: 1981).

Keppel, Robert, *The Riverman—Ted Bundy and I Hunt for the Green River Killer* (Pocket Books: revised edition 2005) and *Signature Killers* (Pocket Books: 1997).

Larsen, Richard W., *The Deliberate Stranger* (Pocket Books: 1980).

MacPherson, Myra, "The Roots of Evil," *Vanity Fair,* May 1989.

Michaud, Stephen G. and Aynesworth, Hugh, *The Only Living Witness* (Signet: 1989) and *Ted Bundy: Conversations with a Killer* (Authorlink Press: 2000).

Nelson, Polly, *Defending the Devil* (William Morrow and Company, Inc: 1994).

Rule, Ann, *The Stranger Beside Me* (Penguin: 20th anniversary edition 2001.

Strong, Marilee, *Erased—Missing Women, Murdered Wives.* (Jossey-Bass: 2009).

U.S. Department of Justice, Federal Bureau of Investigation. Ted Bundy Multiagency Investigative Team Report 1992.

Kivenson-Baron, Inbal, "Fearlessness in Preschoolers: An Extreme End of the Approach and Withdrawal Temperamental Dimension," University of Haifa Faculty of Education, Haifa, Israel, 2010.

Seattle Times, Tacoma News Tribune, Seattle Post-Intelligencer.

Chapter 10

Interviews with Beverly Burr, Julie Burr, Raleigh Burr, Bonnie Taschler, Dick Zatkovich, Ted Strand, Kay Kenwisher, Sandi Holt, Eddie Cavallo, and Yvonne Doherty.

Tacoma Police Department, Missing Person Report on Ann Marie Burr, case #176685, August 31, 1961 – October 16, 1967.

Tacoma News Tribune, The Oregonian, Spokesman Review, Spokane Daily Chronicle, The Oklahoman.

Oklahoma Department of Corrections, Oklahoma State Penitentiary United States Department of Justice, Bureau of Prisons.

Chapter 11

Interviews with: Beverly Burr, Polly Nelson, Dorothy Otnow Lewis, Ann Rule, Bob Keppel, Neil Chethik, Linda Bussey, Edna Martin, Ronald Holmes, Stephen Michaud, Hugh Aynesworth, Chuck Doud, Russ Cor mack, and Bill Hagmaier.

Gladwell, Malcolm, "Damaged," *The New Yorker,* February 24, 1997.

Gladwell, Malcolm, "Something Borrowed," *The New Yorker,* November 22, 2004.

Keppel, Robert, *The Riverman—Ted Bundy and I Hunt for the Green River Killer* (Pocket Books: revised edition 2005) and *Signature Killers* (Pocket Books: 1997).

Larsen, Richard W., *The Deliberate Stranger* (Pocket Books: 1980).

MacPherson, Myra, "The Roots of Evil," *Vanity Fair,* May 1989.

Michaud, Stephen G. and Aynesworth, Hugh, *The Only Living Witness* (Signet: 1989) and *Ted Bundy: Conversations with a Killer* (Authorlink Press: 2000).

Nelson, Polly, *Defending the Devil* (William Morrow and Company, Inc: 1994).

Rule, Ann, *The Stranger Beside Me* (Penguin: 20th anniversary edition 2001).

Minnesota Law Review, Fall, 2005 volumes 67-68.

Brief on Appeal and Application for Stay of Execution, Theodore Robert Bundy v. State of Florida, January 20, 1989.

Deposition of Dr. Emanuel Tanay, Dec. 12, 1987, Psychiatric Evaluation of Ted Bundy, December 12, 1987.

Testimony of Dr. Dorothy Otnow Lewis, Dec. 15, 1987, Psychiatric Evaluation of Ted Bundy. Supreme Court of Florida, Theodore Robert Bundy vs. State of Florida, Brief on Appeal and Application for Stay of Execution, January 20, 1989.

Supreme Court of Florida, Theodore Robert Bundy vs. State of Florida, Denial of Application for Stay of Execution, January 20, 1989.

Fatal Addiction: Ted Bundy's Final Interview, Dobson, Dr. James, January 23, 1989.

The Gainesville Sun, News Tribune, Seattle Post-Intelligencer, Seattle Times.

Inside the Killer's Mind, A&E Investigative Reports, 2000.

Ted Bundy, A&E Biography, 2002.

Ted Bundy—The Mind of a Killer, A&E Biography, 1995.

The Deliberate Stranger, 1986.

The Stranger Beside Me, 2003.

Tacoma News Tribune, Seattle Times, Seattle Post-Intelligencer.

Chapter 12.

Interviews with: Beverly Burr, Julie Burr, Ted Strand, Dick Zatkovich, Raleigh Burr, Bonnie Taschler, and Yvonne Doherty.

MacPherson, Myra, "*The Roots of Evil*," *Vanity Fair*, May 1989.

The New York Times, Seattle Times, Seattle Post-Intelligencer, News Tribune.

Chapter 13

Interviews with: Beverly Burr, Raleigh Burr, Bonnie Taschler, Julie Burr, Laura Hinkel, Edna Martin, Linda Bussey, Sandi Holt, Jerry Bullat, Betty Drost, Ted Strand, Dick Zatkovich, and Yvonne Doherty.

Tacoma Police Department, Missing Person Report on Ann Marie Burr, case #176685, August 31, 1961–October 16, 1967.

Boss, Pauline *Loss, Trauma, and Resilience* (W.W. Norton & Company: 2006) and *Ambiguous Loss* (Harvard University Press: 2000).

MacPherson, Myra, "The Roots of Evil," *Vanity Fair,* May 1989.

The News Tribune, The Oklahoman.

Oklahoma Department of Corrections, Oklahoma State Penitentiary.

United States Department of Justice, Bureau of Prisons.

Chapter 14

Interviews with: Beverly Burr, Julie Burr, Linda Bussey, Bob Keppel, Stephen Michaud, Hugh Aynesworth, Ann Rule, Polly Nelson, Dr. Dorothy Otnow Lewis, Edna Martin, Bill Hagmaier, and Dr. Kent Kiehl.

Ascione, Frank R. "Animal Abuse and Youth Violence," U.S. Department of Justice, Office of Juvenile Justice and Delinquency Prevention, 2002.

Institute for Family Violence Studies, Tallahassee, FL *Competency-Based Training Manual for Animal Abuse Investigators (The Link Between Animal and Human Abuse),* 2000.

Hare, Robert D. PhD *Without Conscience* (The Guilford Press: 1999).

Keppel, Robert *The Riverman—Ted Bundy and I Hunt for the Green River Killer* (Pocket Books: revised edition 2005) and *Signature Killers* (Pocket Books: 1997).

Lewis, Dorothy Otnow M.D. and others, "Objective Documentation of Child Abuse and Dissociation in 12 Murderers with Dissociative Identity Disorder," American Journal of Psychiatry, 154:12, December, 1997.

Lewis, Dorothy Otnow M.D. and others, "Ethics Questions Raised by the Neuropsychiatric, Neuropsychological, Educational, Developmental, and Family Characteristics of 18 Juveniles Awaiting Execution in Texas," *The Journal of the American Academy of Psychiatry and the Law,* 32:408-29, 2004.

Magid, Ken and McKelvey, Carole A. *High Risk: Children Without A Conscience* (Bantam: 1989).

Michaud, Stephen G. and Aynesworth, Hugh, *The Only Living Witness* (Signet: 1989) and *Ted Bundy: Conversations with a Killer* (Authorlink Press: 2000).

Miller, Greg, "Investigating the Psychopathic Mind," *Science,* September 5, 2008.

Nelson, Polly, *Defending the Devil* (William Morrow and Company, Inc: 1994).

Pincus, Jonathan M.D., *Base Instincts—What Makes Killers Kill?* W.W. Norton: 2001).

Ronson, Jon *The Psychopath Test* (Riverhead: 2011).

Rule, Ann, *The Stranger Beside Me* (Penguin: 20th anniversary edition 2001).

Bloom, Paul, "The Moral Life of Babies," *The New York Times Magazine,* May 9, 2010. Seabrook, John,

"Suffering Souls," *The New Yorker*, November 10, 2008.

Chapter 15

Interviews with: Beverly Burr, Julie Burr, Raleigh Burr, Bonnie Taschler, Sandi Holt, Bob Keppel, Ann Rule, Ted Strand, Dick Zatkovich, Bill Hagmaier, Betty Drost, Edna Martin, Jeff Leach, Linda Bussey, and Robert Bruzas.

Tacoma Police Department, Missing Person Report on Ann Marie Burr, case #176685, August 31, 1961–October 16, 1967.

Cour, Robert, "Can You Help Find Anne Marie Burr?" *Master Detective*, April, 1966.

Michaud, Stephen G. and Aynesworth, Hugh, *The Only Living Witness* (Signet: 1989) and *Ted Bundy: Conversations with a Killer* (Authorlink Press: 2000).

Nelson, Polly, *Defending the Devil* (William Morrow and Company, Inc: 1994).

Pincus, Jonathan M.D., *Base Instincts—What Makes Killers Kill?* (W.W. Norton: 2001).

Rule, Ann, *The Stranger Beside Me* (Penguin: 20th anniversary edition 2001).

The News Tribune, Seattle Times, Seattle Post-Intelligencer.

Selected Bibliography

Books

Boss, Pauline *Loss, Trauma, and Resilience* (W.W. Norton & Company: 2006) and *Ambiguous Loss* (Harvard Univer sity Press: 2000).

Capote, Truman *In Cold Blood* (Random House: 1965). Cullen, Dave *Columbine* (Twelve: 2009).

Fiset, Louis *Camp Harmony—Seattle's Japanese Americans and the Puyallup Assembly Center* (University of Illinois Press: 2009).

Fox, James Alan and Levin, Jack *The Will to Kill—Making Sense of Senseless Murder* (Allyn & Bacon: 2001).

Gallacci, Caroline and the Tacoma Historical Society *Old Tacoma* (Arcadia Publishing: 2006) and with Karabaich, Ron *Tacoma's Waterfront* (Arcadia Publishing: 2006).

Hare, Robert D. PhD *Without Conscience* (The Guilford Press: 1999).

Holmes, Ronald M. and Holmes, Stephen T. *Contemporary Perspective on Serial Murder* (Sage Publications: 1998) and *Sex Crimes: Patterns and Behavior* (Sage Publications: 2008).

Kendall, Elizabeth *The Phantom Prince—My Life With Ted Bundy* (Madrona Publishers: 1981).

Keppel, Robert *The Riverman—Ted Bundy and I Hunt for the Green River Killer* (Pocket Books: revised edition 2005) and *Signature Killers* (Pocket Books: 1997).

Larsen, Richard W. *The Deliberate Stranger* (Pocket Book 1980).

Lehr, Dick and Zuckoff, Mitchell, *Judgment Ridge* (Perennial: 2004).

Lewis, Dorothy Otnow M.D. *Guilty By Reason of Insanity* (Ivy Books: 1998).

Magid, Ken and McKelvey, Carole A. *High Risk: Children Without A Conscience* (Bantam: 1989).

March, William *The Bad Seed* (Rinehart: 1954).

Michaud, Stephen G. and Aynesworth, Hugh *The Only Living Witness* (Signet: 1989) and *Ted Bundy: Conversations with a Killer* (Authorlink Press: 2000).

Morgan, Murray *Puget's Sound—A Narrative of Early Tacoma and the Southern Sound* (University of Washington Press: Columbia Northwest Classics edition 2003), and *Skid Road Seattle* (Ballantine Books: fourth printing 1973).

Nelson, Polly *Defending the Devil* (William Morrow and Company, Inc: 1994).

Norris, Joel *Serial Killers* (Anchor Books: 1989).

Olsen, Gregg *If Loving You Is Wrong* (St. Martin's: 1999).

Pincus, Jonathan M.D. *Base Instincts—What Makes Killers Kill*? (W.W. Norton: 2001).

Ronson, Jon *The Psychopath Test* (Riverhead: 2011).

Rosenbaum, Ron *The Secret Parts of Fortune* (Random House: 2000).

Rule, Ann *The Stranger Beside Me* (Penguin: 20th anniversary edition 2001) and *Small Sacrifices* (Penguin: 1988).

Strong, Marilee *Erased—Missing Women, Murdered Wives* (Jossey-Bass: 2009).

Winn, Steven and Merrill, David *Ted Bundy: The Killer* Next Door (Bantam: 1980).

Vronsky, Peter *Serial Killers—The Method and Madness of Monsters* (Berkley Books: 2004).

Articles

Ascione, Frank R. "Animal Abuse and Youth Violence," U.S. Department of Justice, Office of Juvenile Justice and Delinquency Prevention, 2002.

Carson, Richard, "Incredible Affairs of Dr. Boehme," *True Detective*, May, 1966.

Gladwell, Malcolm "Damaged," *The New Yorker*, February 24, 1997, and "Something Borrowed," *The New Yorker*, November 22, 2004.

Kivenson-Baron, Inbal "Fearlessness in Preschoolers: An Extreme End of the Approach and

Withdrawal Temperamental Dimension," University of Haifa Faculty of Education, Haifa, Israel, 2010.

Lewis, Dorothy Otnow M.D. and others, "Objective Documentation of Child Abuse and Dissociation in 12 Murderers with Dissociative Identity Disorder,"American Journal of Psychiatry, 154: 12, December, 1997.

Lewis, Dorothy Otnow M.D. and others, "Ethics Questions Raised by the Neuropsychiatric, Neuropsychological, Educational, Developmental, and Family Characteristics of 18 Juveniles Awaiting Execution in Texas," *The Journal of the American Academy of Psychiatry and the Law,* 32:408-29, 2004.

MacPherson, Myra "The Roots of Evil," *Vanity Fair,* May, 1989.

McDowell, George F., "Let Me Lead You To His Grave," *Startling Detective,* March, 1965.

Miller, Greg, "Investigating the Psychopathic Mind," *Science,* September 5, 2008.

Morgan, Murray "Murray's People," Tacoma Public Library Northwest Room.

Seabrook, John, "Suffering Souls," *The New Yorker,* November 10, 2008.

White, Hal, "Rendezvous With A Corpse" *True Detective,* February, 1961.

Documentaries

Ted Bundy—The Mind of a Killer, A&E Biography, 1995.

Inside the Killer's Mind, A&E Investigative Reports, 2000.

Ted Bundy, A&E Biography, 2002.

Feature Films

The Deliberate Stranger, 1986.

The Stranger Beside Me, 2003.

Audio Recordings and Transcriptions

Conversations between King County Detective Robert Keppel and Ted Bundy, recorded 1989.

Michaud, Stephen G. and Aynesworth, Hugh *Ted Bundy: Conversations with a Killer* (Authorlink Press: 2000).

Documents

Tacoma Police Department, Missing Person Report on Ann Marie Burr, case #176685, August 31, 1961–October 16, 1967.

U.S. Department of Justice, Federal Bureau of Investigation. Ted Bundy Multiagency Investigative Team Report, 1992.

Federal Bureau of Investigation, Freedom of Information and Privacy Acts, Ted Bundy.

Oklahoma Department of Corrections, Criminal Record of Richard Raymond McLish, 1950-1973.

Institute for Family Violence Studies, Tallahassee, FL *Competency-Based Training Manual for Animal Abuse Investigators (The Link Between Animal and Human Abuse)*, 2000.

Court Documents

Deposition of Dr. Emanuel Tanay, Dec. 12, 1987, Psychiatric Evaluation of Ted Bundy, December 12, 1987.

Testimony of Dr. Dorothy Otnow Lewis, Dec. 15, 1987, Psychiatric Evaluation of Ted Bundy.

Supreme Court of Florida, Theodore Robert Bundy vs. State of Florida, Brief on Appeal and Application for Stay of Execution, January 20, 1989.

Supreme Court of Florida, Theodore Robert Bundy vs. State of Florida, Denial of Application for Stay of Execution, January 20, 1989.

Acknowledgments

THERE IS A SAYING THAT JOURNALISM IS THE FIRST rough draft of history. This book would not have been possible without the work of reporters who covered the disappearance of Ann Marie Burr and the crimes of Ted Bundy over the last 50 years. I especially want to acknowledge the reporting of: Chuck Doud, Russ Carmack, Cheryl Reid, Stacey Mulick, Don Hannula, Pat Winkler, Jack Pyle, Lila Fujimoto, Mark Higgins, Dick Monaghan, Greg Heberlein, and Gary Larson of the *Tacoma News Tribune;* Eleanor Bell, Ken Fleming, Herman Hunt, Stan Reed, Bill Prochnau, Arthur C. Gorlick, Robert M. Cour, Michael A. Barber, Gordy Holt, and Steve Miletich of the *Seattle Post-Intelligencer*; Don Duncan, Eric Sorensen, Arthur Santana, and Richard W. Larsen of the *Seattle Times.* Before them, these reporters covered the Tacoma Police Department, the vigilante years of the 1940s and early 1950s, and the careers of Ted Strand and Tony Zatkovich: Jim Faber, Ed Garrison, Larry Shanklin, Paul O. Anderson, Lenny Anderson, and Lee Irwin of the *Tacoma News Tribune*; Burt McMurtrie, of the *Tacoma News Tribune* and the *Tacoma Times;* Sam Angeloff , Robert N. Ward, Murray Morgan, Stub Nelson, Herman Hunt and William Schulze of the *Seattle Post Intelligencer*; Art Burgess of the *Seattle Times*; and Dick Yost, George A. Miller, Carey Wiler, and C.R. Maybin of the *Tacoma Times.* I'm grateful to the *News Tribune* and the *Seattle Times* for the opportunity to use two of the most important and iconic photographs associated with this story: images of the two women at the heart of it, Beverly Burr and Louise Bundy. Thank you to Stephen Michaud and Hugh Aynesworth for permission to quote from their interviews with Ted Bundy, published as *Conversations with a Killer — The Death Row Interviews.*

I'm also indebted to the work of the late Washington state historian Murray Morgan and his research and insights into Tacoma's history.

I have tried to sort the myths from the truth of Ted Bundy's life and the abduction of Ann Marie Burr. There were many. I hope to dispel them.

The use of Beverly Burr's personal letters, essays, and short stories, as well as her photo albums and years of newspaper clippings, were invaluable. Her nephew, Jeff Leach, further expanded the photographic history of the family.

Thank you to Jerry Bullat for memories of his teenage friend, Ted Bundy, and to Sandi Holt, for so bravely sharing her childhood memories, as well as family photos.

I especially thank: Jeanie Fisher, of the Tacoma Public Library; Ann Rule; Gregg Olsen; Raleigh Burr and Bonnie Taschler; Julie Burr; Dick and Susan Zatkovich; and Ted Strand. Dozens of people were interviewed for this book, many more than once. I am very grateful. Thank you: Beverly Burr; Julie Burr; Laura Hinkel; Greg Burr; Raleigh Burr; Bonnie Taschler; Jeff and Pam Leach; Ann Rule; Stephen Michaud; Hugh Aynesworth; Edna Cowell Martin;

Bob Keppel; Polly Nelson; Dr. Dorothy Otnow Lewis; Sandi Holt; Jerry Bullat; Dr. Ronald Holmes; Bill Hagmaier; Chuck Doud; Russ Carmack; Neil Chethik; Kay Kenwisher; Linda Bussey; Betty Drost; Robert Bruzas; Fran Bruzas Trierweiler; Roland Otis; Dick and Susan Zatkovich; Ted Strand; Patricia Strand Jerkovich; Katherine Sauriol; Yvonne Doherty; Eddie Cavallo; Dr. Kent Kiehl; Ron Magden; and Michael Sullivan.

Thank you also to: Elizabeth Steele and the Portland, Ore. office of the FBI; Ed Nolan and the staff of the Tacoma History Museum; the Washington State Historical Society; Tacoma Police Department; author Leslie Rule; The Omaha Public Library; the Oklahoma Department of Corrections; The University of Puget Sound; Sharon Berg; Adrienne Miller of Dog Ear Publishing; and the staff at the Greenwood branch of the Seattle Public Library, the best place to write in all of Seattle.

It was psychotherapist and author Dr. Pauline Boss' studies on ambiguous loss which led to my articles on the Burr family in 2007 and 2008 and my relationship with Beverly Burr. Thanks to family and friends, especially Sterling Morris, Gregg Olsen, Margret Murphy, Bernice Gotta, and Lee Buxton. Whitney Anspach and journalists Ginger Adams Otis and Shirleen Holt shared their wisdom and important editorial advice. Deanah Watson and Brad Arnesen guided me through the myriad of technological decisions an author faces these days.

I'll never forget Bev Burr. I think of her, and of Ann, often.

About the Author

Rebecca Morris is an award-winning journalist who has worked in radio and television news in New York City; Portland, Oregon; and Seattle, Washington. A native Oregonian, her reporting has appeared in *The Seattle Times, The Oregonian, People, Entertainment Weekly,* and many other publications. She lives in Seattle.

To contact her and read more about her work, please go to:

www.RebeccaTMorris.com

Author photograph taken at Couth Buzzard Books in Seattle by Sharon Berg.

Made in the USA
Monee, IL
18 November 2019